WE CAN
SAVE
THE
WORLD

KASHINATH PADHIARY

PARTRIDGE

To order additional copies of this book, contact
Partridge India
000 800 919 0634 (Call Free)
+91 000 80091 90634 (Outside India)
orders.india@partridgepublishing.com

www.partridgepublishing.com/india

CONTENTS

Section-A Introduction

Section-B Acquisition

Section-C Maintainance

Section-D Disposal

Section-E Saving Energy

PREFACE

The earth is changing all the time. This change is natural. Because of these changes (weathering), soil was produced. In the beginning plants grew on these soils and then the animal kingdom came up. Human being appeared last in the process of evolution. Man differed from other animals for its intelligence. By using his intelligence, he learnt the use of fire, though all other animals are afraid of fire. Use of fire simplified his living. He extracted metals, made equipment and learnt cultivation. With this the agricultural revolution started. Until that time very few things were required by man. Few metal objects were used. Mostly man used plant and animal products. Population was less, resources were plenty. So, the environment on the surface of earth did not change much. But with industrial revolution, there were requirement for plenty of raw materials. These raw materials were either obtained from plants, animals or from minerals. Minerals were excavated by mining. Development of industries became a symbol of development and prosperity. More the industries, more the nation was considered developed. There was competition between the countries to develop various industries. Man started living comfortably. Instead of depending on his own physical power or animal power, man depended on machines to do his everyday work. Huge number of things were produced from the industries which ultimately reached the market. People started buying them and threw them out only after a few uses. The concept of disposability made the matter worse. Lot of things was to be produced and were thrown away after a single use or after a few uses only. This produced a huge amount waste material. Use of plastic simplified living, but generated a large amount of non-biodegradable wastes. In the process of mining, extraction of minerals and other industrial activities and generation of wastes altered the earth surface tremendously. Now it has reached such a state that many species of animals and birds have become extinct. Even now it has threatened the human existence. So, it is required to protect the earth for the existence of human beings and other creatures too. As the basic cause of deterioration is increased extraction of natural resources (animal, plant or mineral), so our target should be to reduce extraction of these natural resources. We all have to decrease our demand on the goods we need. We should acquire only those things which we really need. At the same time instead of throwing away after one or two uses, we must use things as long as we can. After our articles lose functioning, we should try to repair them and use again, instead of buying a new one. All these will reduce the demand on new things. After these things are damaged beyond repair, we should try to recycle the material as a whole or in part so that there will be less demand on new minerals. It should be practiced by one and all. Then only this earth can be saved. I have discussed in detail how to execute them or practice them in our daily life. Things are very simple; only we have to be determined to put them into action sincerely. I hope the book will be useful to everyone.

Kashinath Padhiary
Author

DEDICATION

I was born in a remote village in 1957. At that time the economic condition of the people there was very poor, including ours own. The people in the village adopted various means to sustain their livelihood. Mostly they were dependent on sustenance agriculture. They had very few things in their house. They took care of everything they had; in such a way that they used the same thing for several years. They did not waste anything. In almost every house there were several handy machines. Each one of them knew to use them and they could repair a lot of things themselves. Each one of them was a mechanic. If they could not repair, they replace themselves with alternative things (innovated themselves). By that their article continued to give them service. After 50years I feel that they led a life which was truly environment friendly. Hence, I dedicate this book to the then people of my village.

SECTION-A

INTRODUCTION

1

WHY THE EARTH NEEDS TO BE SAVED?

Earth is a unique planet in the universe because lives in different forms exist here. We do not know whether life exists in any other heavenly body or not. There are innumerable varieties of plants and animals here. It is not known what their individual role for the existence of earth is. But almost all are interdependent. The first life forms to appear were the unicellular organisms; followed by the plants. Later in the process of evolution animals arose and last are the human beings. Human beings are different from others in the sense that they can think and alter the environment to its requirements. All other animals live according to the environmental conditions. Either they adjust and survive or they perish. Many cannot adjust and hence they are destined to be extinct. In fact, many have become extinct. Thousands of years have passed after man appeared on the earth. Other animals have been left behind (left where they were); but man has advanced a lot. It has selfishly utilized the natural resources for its comfort without considering much how this will affect the survival of other creatures. In this process it has altered the existing natural environment on the earth. With industrialization the environmental degradation hastened. The environmental factors that are affected are the pollution of water, air and land. In addition to them, the overall temperature of earth has gone up (global warming). If the environment deteriorates in this way, day may come; it may be impossible for men to survive here. If the environmental condition of the earth has to be saved, then only life on earth will be possible; otherwise, it may become a barren land. This can be done by men only. To save the earth from such a situation many country-heads, environmentalists, geologist and scientists have put their heads together. No doubt some progresses have been made; but much more has to be done. Many things can be done at the individual level also. This is what I am going to discuss in this book. If every individual realizes its importance and works accordingly; certainly, earth can be saved from further deterioration and the lost status can be regained to some extent.

2

THE NATURAL RESOURCES

The world is full of natural resources. Man has developed the mechanisms to extract the natural resources and convert them into different useful things. These things have simplified the living of human beings. In all these processes man has altered the earth and its environment also. Up to a certain limit it is not harmful for the living beings on earth. But too much alteration of the environment has been responsible for extinction of several plants and animals.

The resources available on earth can be broadly classified into living and non-living. In the living group there are plants and animals. There are several species of plants and animals. We do not know their role in maintaining the healthy environment on the earth. We cannot take steps to destroy them just because they appear to harm the life or properties of human beings. By doing so, we might be doing greater harm to ourselves than it is apparent. We get many resources from these plants and animals. The important aspect about plants and animals is that they die and the new forms take their place. There is no harm if we only utilize the resources derived from the dead plants or animals. But very often we kill them prematurely to get these resources. At times we do not give enough time for replenishment of these plant and animal resources. At times we do not give any time at all. Not that all animal or plant resources are essential for us. Many are used as luxury and for fun. These activities lead to depletion of plant and animal resources.

The non-living resources on earth are mostly present in the form of minerals. They are present in the mines. We have extracted several minerals for our need. There are three main processes involved in utilization of the mineral resources. The first step is mining which involves digging ores from the mines. The second step is the extraction of the metal from the ores. The third step is converting metals to different articles in various industries. At each step environment is altered in different ways. Earth has been compartmentalized in to different countries. Though for nature earth is one but man has been responsible for such compartmentalization. Its air and water are not limited to any country. Different countries extract the natural resources in different amounts and degrade the environment at variable rate. At times it becomes harmful for other countries or to the whole earth. Industries also utilize plant and animal resources to produce many things.

Several things are manufactured from plants, animals or minerals. Some of the items are essential, some are necessary, some are for comfort and yet some are purely for luxury. It has been described in spiritual scriptures that nature has enough for human needs, but not enough for human greed. It is human greed to have so many things, which is the main cause of deterioration of environment on earth. For example- if we overuse the plant resources, we have to cut down many plants. This will lead to deforestation. If we overuse the animal resources, the animals will be extinct. Though plants or animal resources can be replenished; but it has got a time frame in which it can be replenished. If the extraction becomes faster than it can be replaced it will lead to extinction of the plant or animal. If we overuse the minerals, not only the mineral resources will be exhausted but also it will lead to alteration of the air, water and land ecosystem.

It is also to be remembered that the natural resources can only be utilized by human beings, not by any animal. Hence it is only the human being who can destroy the environment. To save the environment, we have to put a dividing line between our need and greed. This line is not obvious. Everybody has to understand the problem and put his own dividing line. If thought seriously and acted judiciously, man can save the environment. Though the plant and animal resources can be replenished to some extent; but the mineral resources cannot be replenished at all. Man cannot make a mine, possibly nature also cannot make a mine again. However, the environment altered in the process of utilization of mineral resources makes the earth not conducible for existence of living forms.

- Let us see how the animal and plant resources are used.

The flow of living materials (plant or animal derived) is-
First level- Natural plants and animals,
Second level- Industries prepare products from plant or animal resources,
Third level- Users (Man uses the things so prepared),
Fourth level- Rubbish (thrown out here and there by men after use),
Fifth level- The nature degrades them and reutilizes to make new plants or animals.

Nature->Plants/animals-> Industries-> Users-> Nature-> Plants/animals

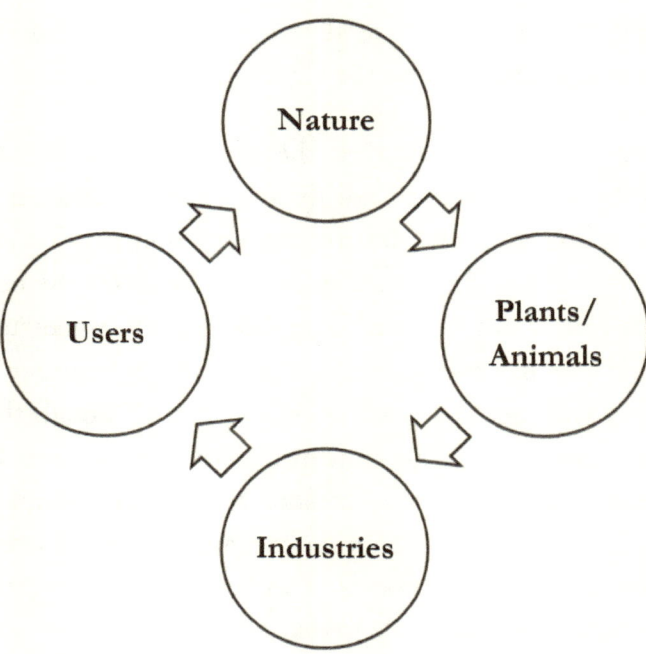

- Similarly let us discuss the path taken by mineral resources while being used.

Flow of mineral resources is mostly unidirectional.
First level- Mines,
Second level-Industries,
Third level- Users,
Fourth level- Dispersed here and there on the earth surface;
The fifth level- Does not exist.
Mines-> Industries-> users-> thrown away here and there (Junk).

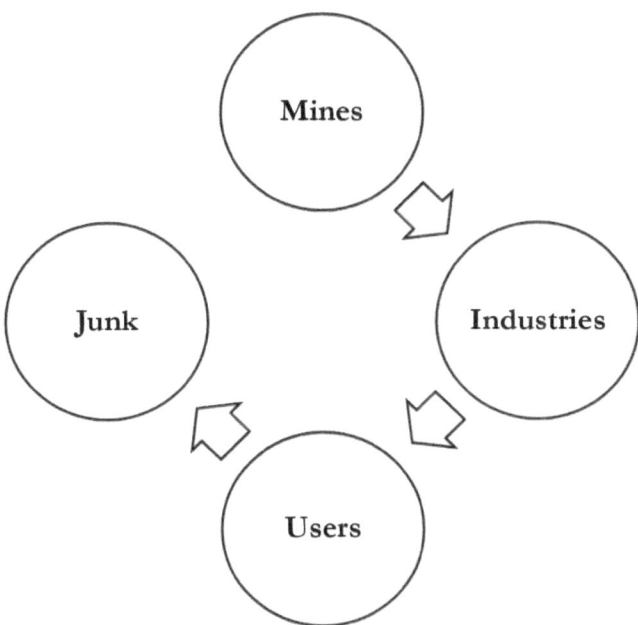

Hence this cycle is incomplete. Only man has to work himself as the fifth level worker and can partly complete the cycle. Nobody can gather the thrown away small pieces of metals together and reassemble to form a mine. But certainly, they can be recycled back to the industry level. More efficient the recycling system, less will be the demand on mines. Less the mining, less will be the mining related degradation of earth's environment. Hence to maintain the natural resources man should -

- Limit the use of plants and animal products so that requirement can always be balanced with replenishment.
- Limit the use of mineral products and should see that the maximum amount of mineral products be recycled back to the industry level to be reutilized (cannot be recycled back to the mine level).

At all these levels every individual has a role to play. An individual can take steps at the level of acquiring things, at the level of maintaining things and finally at the level of disposal of the things.

SECTION-B

ACQUISITION

3

HOUSE

We require a house to live. An ideal house should provide us shelter during different seasons. It should provide place to prepare food, to store food/food grains and should provide place to sleep and sit. We require houses of different sizes to meet all these requirements. Either we may construct our house or we may buy a readymade house. Often people make big houses which is very often not required. If we can manage with a two roomed house, there is no need to buy a four roomed or ten roomed house. The materials to be used for the extra space can be considered as wastage of natural resources. If we can manage with an apartment there is no need of an independent house. If we construct a small house or be satisfied with an apartment, we can save space. This saved space can be utilized for agriculture or animal rearing. Constructing a bigger house than actual requirement leads to wastage of space for other activities like animal rearing, agriculture. Similarly, we can limit the interior furnishing required for us. Luxurious interior furnishing just for fashion can lead to loss of natural resources and it might be expensive too. Very often it is not required. Hence, we should construct such a house which is exactly required for us. By that we can save a lot of natural resources. There are many important people on earth who are still living in small houses even if they have the capability to construct a big house. In the Bible also it is described that man should build simple shelters. (The Old Testament, Leviticus; The festivals of shelters). Once we build a house, it should be maintained properly, so that it will require very little repair and it will last for a long time. Frequent repair or reconstruction of the house will also lead to the wastage of natural resources. One should remember that water is the most important thing that brings damage to a house. Hence, we should see that there is no water logging or water leakage anywhere in our house. Besides water, the white-ants also act as great enemy to wooden fittings in a house. We should build a termite-resistant house at the time of construction or use anti-termite treatment from time to time. We shall discuss how to take care of other household things separately.

4

CLOTHES

We require different types of clothes for different purposes; clothes for office, clothes for festive occasions and clothes to be used in domestic set up. Different types of clothes are also required in different seasons. In relation to clothes and environment the following points are to be noted.

- If we can manage with five sets of dresses, we need not accumulate twenty sets of dresses. The clothes that we wear are derived from plant or animal products. Less we require less is the requirement of these plant or animal products. If we have acquired large numbers of clothes, very often they remain under-utilized.
- If we can manage with a half sleeve shirt, there is no need to have full sleeve shirts. This is particularly true in tropical countries.
- If we can manage with half pants, there is no meaning in wasting the natural resources in making full pants.
- We should take proper care of our clothes so that they are not damaged by insects or by other means.

- We should clean each cloth as per the instructions of the manufacturer; otherwise, it may get damaged and its color may get distorted also.
- We should wear such clothes that are comfortable to us; we should not get carried away by fashion. If the fashion changes, our dress will become useless. This leads to misuse of natural resources. So proper selection and maintenance of our clothes can save a lot of natural resources.

5

SHOES

Shoes are made of animal hides or of synthetic materials. If we use so many shoes or damage so many shoes due to lack of proper care; it will increase demand on these resources. Some of the points discussed below can help one to choose his shoes.

- While buying shoes we should see that they fit well. The shoes which do not fit us well, may get rejected after using for a short time only. Hence it is wasted.
- Shoes for occasional use should be different from those for regular use.
- Waterproof shoes should be used in the rainy season. If a leather shoe gets wet, it should be dried immediately.
- We should buy shoes with minimum stitches and few crevices. These are the weak points in a shoe. Often the shoe gets torn from these places. Dirt also accumulates easily at these points.
- If the shoes get torn, we should mend it quickly, provided the overall condition of the shoe is good. If the overall condition of the shoe is too bad, it is better to discard it and buy a new one.

- Like the clothes, there is no need of buying several pairs of shoes. A few are enough.
- By limiting the number of shoes, we can reduce the burden on natural resources.

6

FOOD

Food has a significant role in contributing to the worsening environmental condition on the earth. The huge human population, the amount of food required for them, the choice of food, food being taken as luxury item (instead of an essential item), commercial production of food; all have led to the deterioration of earth's environment.

Let us discuss these points in detail.

Amount of food- How much food we are supposed to take? To understand this, we should have some knowledge about the scientific aspects of food. We take food to get energy. We need energy to do our activities. Majority of the life activities at cellular level require energy. Some of the work done at organ level; like respiratory movement, digestion, absorption, circulation of blood, pumping of the heart; all require energy. Thinking of brain also requires energy. We do some daily activities like eating, talking, passing urine, defecating; all become possible due to contraction of certain muscles. This requires energy. Regulation of body temperature also requires energy (Human beings have a fixed internal body temperature). Life cannot be sustained unless we provide energy for these purposes. Energy in biological system is calculated as calories and kilo-calories. One calorie is that much of energy that is required to raise the temperature of 1gm of water from 15 to 16⁰C. This is a very small amount of energy. Hence for practical purposes we use kilo-calories which is 1000times the value of one calorie. For basal metabolism an adult of 60Kg requires about 1400kilo-calories (Kcal). If we convert it into a meal- 400gm of cereals or 2liters of milk can provide this much of calories. Basal metabolism means the amount of energy required to maintain all life activities like respiration, circulation, digestion, urination and defecation etc. (no physical activity is included). Extra energy is needed for physical activities. The amount varies depending on the severity of physical activities. We should know that one gm of carbohydrate gives 4Kcal; 1gm of protein gives 4Kcal and one gm of fat gives 9Kcal. For survival we require all these three types food in different proportion at different ages. Extra calories are needed as per our physical activities. More vigorous the work and longer the duration of work; more is the requirement of energy. A man doing very hard work may require about 2600kcal. If we take more calories (means more food) but do not use them for doing physical work, it remains unutilized and it is converted into fat. The extra fat gets deposited in different parts of the body; particularly around our waste line. We become obese. Obesity is a major risk factor for several diseases like diabetes, hypertension, heart diseases etc. That is why it has been told that waste line decreases life line. Hence, we should take that much of food to maintain the ideal body weight. Ideal body weight (grossly) can be known from the formula; Height in cm - 100 = weight in Kg. In females it is about 2-3Kg less. This calculation is for adults only; not for children. There is different chart to know ideal body weight of children. If we take more food, not only it causes diseases but also it contributes to worsening of the earth's environment. In an attempt to grow more food, we also cause damage to the environment.

- We adopt commercial agriculture.
- We use artificial manure and insecticides.
- We create more cultivable land by cutting down trees (deforestation) or by filling water bodies.

If we all become conscious about the amount of food we should take, there will be surplus food. If less food is required less is to be grown. Hence less will be the damage to the environment. The holy Quran also denies taking food more than required (Annahal, 114-117). Hence, growing less food will maintain better natural environment.

Type of food- We should not be too much concerned about taking a particular food. Some scientific knowledge is also required to understand the type of food we should take. We will discuss this point on several issues.

- *Animal food*-For growth, development and repair protein is required. Protein is made up of amino acids. There are twenty types of amino acids. Out of them eight are essential. They are essential because our body cannot produce them. They have to be taken from outside. Animal protein contains all the essential amino acids. So, they are considered as better-quality proteins. But if cereals and pulses are taken together, we can also get all these amino acids. This means one is not bound to take animal proteins. Vegetarians can get all the essential amino acids if they take cereals and pulses. The main conclusion of this discussion is-in the countries where plants foods (cereals and pulses) are grown in plenty they need not take animal meat and in the countries where plant foods are not available (as in Antarctica), there is no harm in taking animal food. In this regard- Indian spiritual scripture writes- nothing is good food or bad food; food should be decided according to the availability in the locality (discussed later). As such availability depends on the geographic conditions which are not in the hands of man; rather it is in the hands of nature. Hence one should not be too much inclined to take any particular food.

- **_Fruits_**- Very often we buy different fruits which have been imported from other places; at times from other countries. But according to geographical conditions various kinds of fruits are grown in different parts of the world. Almost all fruits have similar nutritional value. If a particular food is chosen by us, it will lead to commercial production of these fruits which will be responsible for deterioration of the environmental conditions. So, fruits should be taken according to the availability in the locality.

Commercial production of food- To meet the growing demand for food, people all over the world started growing crops in commercial scale. Because of open economy and to earn more foreign currency, every country started producing a particular type of food having great demand in international market. Often demand is artificially created by advertisements and by other means. Commercial agriculture required help of machines, use of chemical fertilizers, use of insecticides and other chemicals to preserve the food also. These chemical substances have been responsible for pollution of the environment (land and water). This has led to extinction of different types of insects and worms. These insects and worms are very much required for natural process of biodegradation and for maintaining the food cycle. Man started producing animal food also in commercial scale. I shall give just one example how animal food production in commercial scale became harmful to the society. Some of the European countries fed the cows with fodders mixed with animal proteins. These cows grew well and yielded a lot of good quality beef which helped these countries to export to other countries.

Cows by nature are herbivorous. Feeding them non-vegetarian food was against the law of nature. Within years it was found that this practice was responsible for the development of Mad-cow disease (Benign Spongiform Encephalopathy). It was very easily transmitted via a protein (prion). It did not even require a living organism. The conclusion from this instance is- commercial practice to grow more food (plant or animal) should be restricted and no un-natural methods should be adopted to grow food. Commercial production of food has also led to clearing of forests leading to deforestation. Deforestation is one of the major causes of deterioration of the environmental condition on earth.

Food as luxury- All living beings require three things for survival. These are air, water and food. Plants can produce their own food. But the whole animal kingdom is dependent on the plants for their food (directly or indirectly). Hence food is essential. However, we often go beyond this. We take food as luxury. Here are a few examples.

1. Now- a- days, we are taking food as a luxury item. We take food in different flavors and in different forms. In the process of preparing such foods a lot of oils and other spices are being used. Without clearly knowing how much it will be beneficial to our body; we went on eating them. Because we can pay and because such foods are tasty, we often take them in excess (more than our requirement). Its effect has already been discussed in relation to the amount of food. Animal foods burnt or fried in oil medium generates advanced glycation end (AGE) products which are responsible for several life style diseases.

2. People all over the world consume a lot of coffee and tea, though these are not food at all. Those people, who are not eating them, are not suffering from any problem. For example- the Indians were not taking tea/coffee a few generations back.

It did not cause any problem in them. That means- tea and coffee are not required in our food for healthy living. But liters of them are being consumed within a day by a single individual; not to speak of the total world consumption. If all people will stop taking them from today; consumption will become zero. Once consumption becomes zero, one day production will also become zero. No tea and coffee will be grown. We all know that tea and coffee are grown in hilly areas. If tea and coffee are not grown, within a few years these areas will be covered with forests. This will provide enough space for living of animals, birds and reptiles. Indirectly it can be told that our luxurious food habit is responsible for the extinction of these animals. If tea and coffee consumption cannot be stopped completely; even reducing their intake by half can save at least half of the forest lands.

Food from spiritual angle- Any discussion about food without its spiritual angle will be incomplete. These are some of the points-

- The total amount of food grown on the earth is for all living beings. Man does not have the right to take all. We all know that a monkey does not cultivate, a rat does not grow food and an ant does not have a farm. Then how do they get their food? Nature has arranged food for all. If we take more food than required, there will be deficit for other creatures. If man takes more food, he will become obese. From spiritual angle this means an obese man has stolen the food of other creatures. He is responsible for depriving others of food. Let us discuss this point in detail. Suppose a man is overweight by 20Kg. The amount of fat in this extra 20Kg will be about 12Kg (water content in fatty tissue is less). The calorific value of 12Kg fat will be $9 \times 12 \times 1000 = 1,08,000$Kcal (as one gram of fat gives 9Kcal). A moderately severely working individual requires 2000Kcal per day. This 12Kg fat will amount to food of 52persons (108000/2000=52). This means if a man possesses 20Kg extra weight for one day; he has kept 52people unfed for one day. If he carries this extra weight for one year, (52x365=18980) 18980 people have remained deprived of food. One can well imagine how many birds and animals can be sustained with this much of calories.

- In the Bible it is described that if a farmer plucked grapes from his orchard and a few grapes dropped out of his basket, he should not pick them up. If unknowingly the farmer has left a few bunches in his orchard- he should not return back and pluck them (The Bible, Old Testament, Leviticus, Laws of holiness and justice). God says, "I have kept them hidden from your vision for other animals or for hungry travelers. Even if you have grown them, you have no total right on your produce." In the same scripture (The Bible, Old Testament, Leviticus, laws of holiness and justice) it is described- not to cut corns from the edges of the field, not to harvest olive or grape vines on every seventh year (The Bible, Old Testament, Exodus, The Seventh Year and seventh day)

- In Srimadbhagabat it is described that-
"Ahare bhala Manda Nahin; Je sthane jemanta milai.
Santoshe karai ahara, Tenu bichara nahin mora.
Alape Bahute Santosa, Na mile kare ubapasa."
(Odia Ekadasaskandha, page-64)

This means, "Nothing is good food or bad food; food should be decided according to the availability in the locality. One should eat everything with great satisfaction. He should remain happy whether he gets more food or less. If no food is available, it is wiser to fast than to take food which is not meant for him."

- If we observe the behavior of a monkey eating a mango at the tree top, we can also understand certain principles of food intake existing in nature. It eats from different sides of the mango and then throws it down; still around 30% of the mango not eaten. He never eats till the last gram of the mango is over. But a human being consumes till the last gram of it is over. The portion that he throws down is eaten by insects, worms, ants etc. This is the law of nature. A portion of the food we grow should be left for other creatures.

By discussing so much about food from scientific and spiritual angle, we can conclude that if each of us modify our feeding habit (follow the laws of nature); we can greatly contribute to save the natural environment.

7

VEHICLES

The greatest source of environmental pollution has come from excessive use of vehicles due to burning of fossil fuel. Burning of fossil fuel releases a lot of harmful gases and particulate materials to the atmosphere. This causes several problems like acid rain, global warming etc. Besides these, the other way they bring damage to the environment are due to construction of roads (running of vehicles require better quality roads). In the process a lot of forest lands are cleared and acres of agricultural lands are filled up. Vehicles moving at high speed cause many accidents and kill or cripple many human beings. Many innocent animals and birds are also crushed. To prevent destruction of natural environment by vehicles, we can help in the following ways. We should-

- Use them only when it is a must.
- Use public vehicles as far as possible.
- Use fuel-efficient vehicles.
- Try to have only one vehicle; but in a good condition. Having multiple vehicles not only likely to waste fuel; but also consumes various mineral materials with which these are made. By possessing many vehicles, we put pressure on natural resources.

8

ANIMAL PRODUCTS

Buying animal products needs special mention because several species of animals are quickly becoming extinct. Many people possess animal skins, bones, teeth and other parts just out of fun or as a symbol of aristocracy. These things do not impart any role in our daily living. Because we buy, so the poachers kill these animals. If we all stop buying them (as it is not at all required for our living) they will not kill the animals. Hence, we can contribute to save these animals. If at all we use animal products like shoes, bags, belts, wallets made of leather, we should take their proper care so that they will give service for a long time. By that we will not buy them again and again. We can also limit the number of such items. Instead of accumulating many such items, we should manage with a few only. By doing so, we can reduce the demand on animal products and can prevent unnecessary killing of animals.

9

WATER

Like food, water is an important natural and essential resource. Water means life. Without water life is not possible. Though 75% of the earth surface is covered with water, it is present in oceans and seas. As it is saline in nature, it is of no use to the land plants and land animals including man. They all need fresh water. The only source of fresh water on land is rain water. Rain water is used for domestic purposes as well as in the industries. A large amount of fresh water is also required for agriculture. In the present time the number of crops being grown has increased and the number of industries has also increased. They consume a lot of water. The limited water on land is quickly becoming inadequate. To meet the demands, we all have to conserve rain water. Major part of the rain water is flown away to the sea by the rivers, particularly during heavy rains and flood. Attempt should be made to save this water. Different steps can be taken to conserve fresh water.

At community level-
- We should make several dams across the river to hold water during flood so that it will not be flown into the sea. Water

holding capacity of the rivers can be increased by increasing the height of the embankments.

- We should construct ponds, artificial lakes, ditches or other water bodies of various shapes and sizes to hold water in rainy season. The water bodies that are being filled up by sand or silt should be dug up to increase their water holding capacity.

- Damaged dams and embankments should be quickly repaired to prevent leakage of water.

- If there are wells, they should be filled up during rain. These wells also work as soaking pits to improve the ground water level.

- Water used in irrigation can be minimized by growing such crops which need less water or the method of irrigation can be modified. For example- drip irrigation can be adopted instead of flood irrigation. Drip irrigation consumes less water.

- For cultivation we should use the exact amount of water required for a particular crop. Excess of water may be harmful for certain crops.

At domestic level-

- We require 2-2.5 liters of water to drink in a day. The amount varies depending on the weather. There is no need to take more water.

- If we are washing our clothes in washing machine, we should put clothes to its capacity. Less cloth will waste more water. Choosing clothes for cleaning is also important. We should try to use our dresses for the maximum possible time. It may be our shirts, pants, underwear or bed sheets.

- Domestic waste water can be used for watering plants in our kitchen garden/ back yard.

- We should see that none of our taps or storage units (like overhead tank) or pipe system is leaking. They not only waste water but also bring damage the building.
- If we are flushing our toilet, we should use the minimum possible water to flush; there is no need to flush repeatedly. Flushing after urination requires less water than after defecations.
- It is often seen that people keep the tap flowing while brushing or shaving. It leads to wastage of water. Taps should be kept closed when not in use.
- For cooking also, we should use the required amount of water. Putting more water and then draining out leads to-
  - ➢ Wastage of water.
  - ➢ Wastage of energy used to heat that extra water.
  - ➢ Loss of water-soluble vitamins.

10

OTHER THINGS

There are many more things that are required in our daily life. It will not be possible to discuss about every item. Hence, some general guidelines will be described which can be used while buying/ acquiring new things. Everybody wants to buy new things. But a wise man thinks well before buying anything new. These days various types of articles are available in the market. All are not needed for us. Different advertisements allure us to buy these things. But before buying a new thing, we should consider the following points.

1. **Getting carried away by advertisement**

   Advertisements in TV or newspaper emphasize more on the merit of a thing. The manufacturers do not reveal anything about its demerits or limitations. Often, they write the limitations in very small letters; so small that it cannot be read clearly. In TV they often mention, conditions apply. By mentioning the limitations in this way, they hide many facts.

2. **Actual need of the thing**

   Before buying anything, we should be sure that we really need it. If at all we need it, we should know how we are going to use it. We should also think how it will help in our way of living. Often, we get tempted to buy something because some of our friends or neighbors have got it. We should never compare ourselves with them. Because, they might be requiring it. Their financial status might be different from ours. Even their decision to buy that thing might be wrong also. They might be repenting for their purchase, which they might not be revealing to us. So, we should think clearly (without any bias) whether we need it or not.

3. **The old thing**

If we have a similar old thing and we feel to buy a new one, we have to consider several things too. We should know clearly why are we interested to buy a new one; in what way the new one will give better service than the old one. If the old one is giving proper service, we should not buy a new one; because there is no guarantee that we will get the same service from the new one. The saying "Old is gold" is quite true. There might be marginal advantage of the new thing, but it may not be required for us. If the old one is not giving proper service or giving problems, it should be checked by an experienced mechanic if it can be properly repaired. If the decision is final about buying the new thing, then we should dispose of the old one; either in exchange offer or by selling. Without disposing off the old one and buying a new one means dumping things in our house. Those who are living in apartments there might very limited space. So, it may be difficult to accommodate all these things (old and new) in a small house. It is a common experience that with little maintenance, old things remain useful for several years.

4. The service facility

While buying things we should always look for the post sale service facility. Most of the things will go out of order in due course; at times within a short time from the day of purchase and these will require servicing. The servicing required might be for a very small defect, but for the lack of that the article remains useless. Longer it lies useless more useless it will become. So, for repair we should not run from place to place. Hence, we should buy such a thing that ensures servicing.

5. The best one

It is a common saying that if we are going to use a thing for more than five years, we should buy the best one. There is lot of rationality in it. These are-

- If we buy the best one, we are likely to get good service for coming few years.
- If we buy an old model thing at a low price, after some time it may become completely outdated for which we may have to buy again.
- It may be difficult to get the spare parts later on.

6. Which one to buy

These days several varieties of the same article made by different companies are available in the market. In fact, there are so many varieties that one will be easily confused. But there is little difference between them. We can enquire from our friends who have bought similar things and whether they have experienced any merit or demerit. Often comparative analysis comes out in newspapers and magazines; if possible, we should read them. Always we should look for utility rather than fashion. We may have to pay more just for show purpose. For example- if we see TV for one or two hours in a day, there is no meaning in buying a costly TV. If our primary objective is to receive calls and send messages an ordinary mobile phone is enough, there is no meaning in buying a costly mobile phone. These principles can be applied for almost all household things.

In this regard it can be told again that maintenance of old things is better than buying new things.

If we apply these guidelines and acquire things exactly for our requirement, we can reduce the burden on natural resources.

SECTION-C

MAINTAINANCE

11

IMPORTANCE OF MAINTENANCE

There is a Sanskrit verse which clearly speaks of the importance of maintenance. It is-

> *"Praja sangrakhyati nrupa sa bardhayati parthibam,*
> *Bardhandrakyanam sreyastadabhabe sadapasyat"*
> *(Hitopadesh. Bigraha and Sandhi; Verses: 3; P.136).*

This means out of king and the people in general (subjects), higher place (more importance) has been given to the king. Because people together may build a kingdom, but it is the king who maintains the kingdom. If the king cannot maintain it, the kingdom will collapse within no time. Similarly, out of acquiring new things and maintaining existing things, maintenance has been given more importance; because if a new thing is not maintained properly, it will be damaged within no time.

There are many things in every household. These are made of iron, plastic, aluminium, glass, wood and so on. These are either industrial products or derived from plants. The industrial products are dependent for their manufacture on certain raw materials. These raw materials are derived from certain minerals or from some animal products or some plant products. These products if used for a long period of time, it will decrease the demand on raw materials. Decrease in the demand on the raw materials means preservation of the natural resources. Preservation of the natural resources means saving the environment. Saving the environment will save the earth. Hence the things that I am going to discuss in this section will have maximum impact on conservation of environment and at the same time it will also help in improving personal saving. Let us discuss a few examples.

(a) Suppose person "A" wants to have a cot made of wood. Let its cost be 500 dollars and let the wood comes from one tree. If he takes its proper care, he will use it for 25 years. Similarly, let another person "B" also buys a similar cot. This second person does not take its proper care and the cot is damaged in 5years. This second person has to buy five such cots in 25years. This means "A" has to spend 500 dollars in 25 years and "B" has to spend 2500 dollars during the same time. This amounts to a personal saving of 2000 dollars for "A". In terms of environment "A" is responsible for cutting one tree where as "B" is responsible for cutting 5 trees in these 25 years. So, proper care of all wooden articles can prevent cutting of trees. If this is practiced by all it will mean a lot in terms of saving the environment.

(b) Let us consider about mineral products. Suppose person "A" made an iron gate. Let its weight be 500kgs. By proper care of the gate, he used it for twelve years. If the same gate is used by another person "B" and he does not take proper care. Let it gets damaged within three years. So, he has to build it four times in these twelve years. "B" will spend four times more money than "A". This extra amount is a saving for "A". In terms of environment, "A" is responsible for saving the mineral resources and "B" is responsible for loss of natural resources (minerals).

In this way if all of us handle all our house-hold things carefully and take their proper care, they will last long. It will not be required to buy them again and again. By this we can save money for us and at the same time we can help in saving the natural resources. Saving the natural resources amounts to saving the earth.

12

MAINTENANCE OF HOUSEHOLD THINGS

(A) Glass goods

In every house there are a few things made of glass. The commonly used glass items are tumblers, mirrors, utensils, jugs, table top glass, window panes, spectacles, book shelves, show cases and so on. The weak point of glass goods is- these are easily breakable and they do not withstand high temperature (unless heat resistant). So, one should be careful in handling these things. The factors which can lead to breakage of glass goods are-

- Fall,
- Something striking (external physical force),
- Jerky movement,
- Wide variation in temperature

(i) *Fall:* Glass items often break because of fall. So, while keeping these things, we should see that they do not fall. Some knowledge of physics will help in this regard. The following principles should be adopted to prevent a fall.

- Glass goods should be kept in a stable position. By that it will not fall down with slight movements.

- They should not be put near the margin of a surface like the table top. Slight movement can make them fall.

The Glass on left is correctly placed
The Glass on the right is wrongly placed

- They should be put on a surface which can bear their weight. It is to be remembered that many glass goods are quite heavy.
- They should not be put on an uneven surface; they may turn over.

A wrongly placed glass

- They should not be towed one above the other. This rule should be followed while keeping or carrying them. With slight loss of balance, they can drop and break.

Glasses on the left are correctly placed for carrying
Glass goods on right are wrongly placed for carrying

- If these are kept in a shelf, they should be kept in the lowermost shelf. Because, if at all the article falls, the thrust may not be strong enough to break it. If it falls from a higher shelf, the chances of getting broken will be more.
- If we are hanging glass goods (like a mirror), we should see that the nail can bear its weight and the hook on the back side of the mirror should be in good condition. Defect in any part of them can make the item fall and break.
- While handling a glass object, we should make it a rule to replace it at the earliest in its original place. Very often glass items are broken due to improper placement.

(ii) **Something striking:** Glass goods can break if something strikes them. The common things that can hit them are-

- Things (like a ball) thrown by children inside the house. That can strike glass goods and damage them. So, children should not be allowed to play inside the house. But, we should remember that it is difficult to control children. So, we should give them alternatives to play. Either they should be taken outside for playing outdoor games or they should be given indoor games which does not involve something been thrown.

- Window panes can break by balls from children playing outside. They should be dissuaded from playing near the house. Window panes also break due to striking against the window frame by strong wind. If strong wind is blowing or is likely to blow, the windows should be closed immediately. It may so happen that strong wind blows after we leave the house and cause the damage. So, we should shut all the windows before we leave the house. This is particularly important in summer and rainy season.

- Windscreen or the glass window of a car may break due to striking of things from outside. Some common sites where we should guard are-

    ➢ we should not park our vehicles where children are playing. We should cross the playing arena carefully and as quickly as possible.

    ➢ While going by the side of cattle, we should be careful about their unpredictable movement.

    ➢ We should park our vehicle away from the windows near a multi-storied building. If something is thrown out of the windows, it may fall on our car and can break the glass items.

    ➢ On windy days we should not park our vehicle under the trees. Branches of tree may break and fall on the car.

- One should be attentive while carrying glass items. Otherwise, we ourselves may get hit against something or we may stumble over something and lose balance. This may lead to breakage of the glass goods.

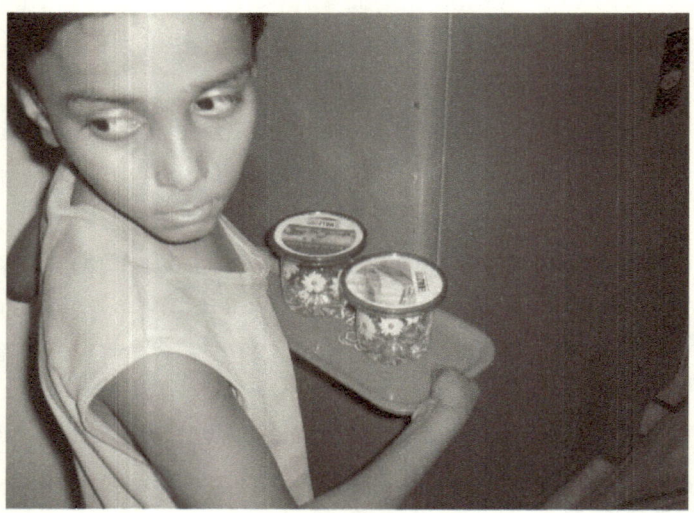

Inattentive while transporting glass goods

This principle has also to be followed while carrying other breakable things.

(iii) Jerky movement: Jerky movement can break glass items, if these are loosely packed or not properly packed. We should prevent jerky movement of the vehicles carrying glass items. Whenever transported they should be packed properly. It is preferable to preserve the packing material in which the glass goods were packed at the time of purchase.

(iv) Extreme variation of temperature: Heat resistant glasses are specially prepared. Except them, all other types of glass items should be carefully handled in relation to heat. We should not-

- Put hot things into a glass object unless it is made of heat resistant glass.
- Put ordinary glass goods directly under the flame or in the oven.

- Put them too near the hot objects or fire.
- Put glass bottles full of water inside the deep freeze. Once the water turns into ice, its volume expands and that can break the bottle.

(B) Wooden goods

In every house there are some wooden goods. Now-a- days wooden goods have become too costly. So, these goods should be properly taken care of. If properly taken care of, wooden goods can last for several years. The threats to wooden goods are the white-ants, water and sun. The following methods can be adopted for proper care of such items. We should-

- See that wooden goods are not exposed to sun for a prolonged period.
- Not allow the wooden goods to remain wet for a long time. Oil painting can protect them from water.
- Polish the wooden goods periodically to maintain their shine and to increase their life span.
- Use the wooden goods regularly. Regular use prevents attack by white-ants. Wooden goods not used for a long time can make them ill-fitting due to change of shape.
- See that they do not touch the ground. Wooden things touching the ground can be damaged by white-ants. If already attacked by white-ants, we should shift the goods to a dry place. If they cannot be shifted, insecticide should be sprayed on them.
- Carefully shift the wooden goods from one place to another. Instead of dragging them on the floor; they should be lifted as a whole and shifted. Dragging on the floor will not only damage the floor but also loosen the legs of furniture.

(C) Iron goods

There are many goods in every household which are made of iron, starting from needles and knives to gates, grills and almirahs. Iron goods are stronger no doubt, but their weak point is rusting. Rusting is a chemical process which occurs in presence of oxygen (air) and water. Lack of any one will not lead to rusting. It is not possible to keep things away from oxygen as it is present everywhere in air, so the only way to prevent rusting is to keep these things away from water. Rusting of iron not only weakens the article but also causes them to malfunction. The following steps can be taken to prevent rusting.

- Iron goods should be regularly used.
- If not in use, they should be coated with oil paint. The coating should be thick enough and should cover every point. If some points are not covered, rusting can start from these points and can damage the iron goods. Outdoor things which are directly exposed to rain and dew (like gates and grills) should be oil-painted more frequently.
- Iron goods that are touching the ground like the legs of almirahs or iron-cots should be prevented from getting wet (as happens while washing the floor). To prevent rusting the legs can be put on plastic pieces or wooden pieces.

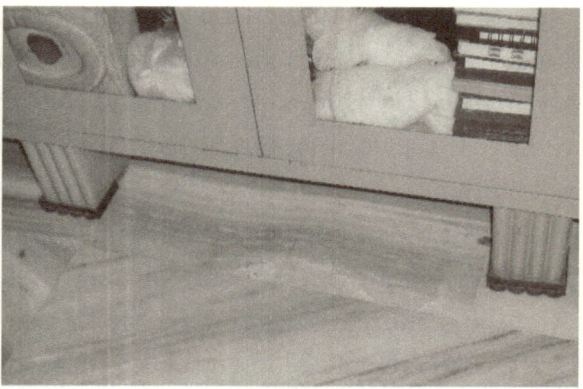

Plastic boots under the legs of an almirah

- Cutting things like axe, knife, and sickle should be coated with oil. Such things should not be oil painted as it will blunt the sharpness.
- Very small things like needles can be directly put inside the oil. The mouth of the container should be wide enough, so that it will be easy to bring them out.
- Iron containers (like utensils and buckets) should be kept dry. If not in use for a long time, they can be coated with oil. These goods should be kept dry and when not in use should be kept upside down.

(D) Aluminium Goods

Every house might be having some aluminium goods also. It may be utensil, bucket, mug and so on. Aluminium does not react with pure water. However, we rarely use pure water. There might be impurities like acidic or alkaline substances mixed with water. These impurities can lead to reaction with aluminium and cause corrosion. Aluminium reacts with air (oxygen) to form aluminium oxide which makes a coating on the surface of such things and prevent corrosion. However repeated scrubbing removes the oxide coat and exposes metallic aluminium to oxygen making a fresh coat. Hence, repeated scrubbing reduces the life span of the aluminium goods. The following methods can be adopted to prevent rusting of aluminium goods. We should-

- Avoid prolonged contact with water. Aluminium pots are not suitable for storing water. If we want to store water, we should prefer pots made of plastic or stainless steel or other alloys like brass.
- Aluminium containers should be kept upside down after washing.

Method to keep an aluminium bucket after use

By that water will be drained out quickly and completely. If kept in the upright position, water will remain at the bottom and rusting will start from those points.

• Even we should not hang aluminium mugs from a nail. Water will trickle to the dependent part and corrosion will start from these points.

An aluminium mug hung in this way can rust at the bottom

Aluminium is a malleable metal; it is not as strong as iron. So, if it falls from a height or if something strikes them, it will get deformed though it will not break like a glass item. So, they should be handled like glass items to prevent denting.

(E) Plastic goods

Plastic things in our houses have replaced many metallic things. Plastic goods are light and water repelling. There are basically two types of plastic goods. The hard plastic goods are breakable like glass and the soft plastic goods do not break easily. Both are not heat resistant, particularly the soft ones. Few plastics like Bakelite and melamine are heat resistant. If properly taken care of plastic goods can last for several years. Some general guidelines on the use of plastic things are-

1. We should not put them directly over flame.
2. We should not keep them too near the fire, unless it is made up of Bakelite or melamine.
3. We should not drop plastic goods from a height particularly if it is already filled with heavy things. In such a situation, even the plastic goods made of soft plastic can also break. For example- if an empty bucket is dropped from a certain height, it will not break; but the same bucket filled with water if dropped, can break.
4. Plastic containers are good to store things, but not good to transport things. For example- if we store water in a plastic bucket for several years, nothing will happen, but carrying water in it can cause damage, particularly at its junctions with the handle. The junction of the handle with the body of the bucket is a weak point. Cracks usually start from these points. If at all heavy things are to be carried,

Weak point of a plastic bucket

they should be carefully carried. We should carry them smoothly and avoid jerky movement. Similarly, if we are carrying heavy things in them, the weight should be distributed over wider area, instead of concentrating at one or two points.

Wrong way to lift a tub full of water   Correct way to lift a tub full of water

5. We should look for the weak points of the plastic things. Most of such things have some weak points from where cracks start. Let us discuss a few.
    *   The weak point of a bucket is its junction of the handle with the body.
    *   The weak point of a mug is the junction of its handle with the body. If we lift the water-filled mug holding solely its handle, the handle will break soon. If we lift by holding the handle along with a part of the body, it will not break easily.

| Wrong way to hold a plastic mug full of water | Correct way to hold a mug full of water |

* The weak point of a plastic chair is the junction of the legs with its seat. We should see that this point is not put under stress. So, plastic chairs should be put on uniformly flat surface. By that the weight will be equally

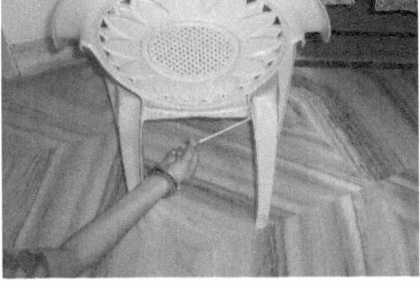

Weak point of a plastic chair

distributed to all the four legs. If they are put on uneven surface, weight will be distributed unequally and one or the other leg will break.

* Many people have the habit of sitting by leaning forward or leaning backward. Here the whole weight of the individual has to be carried on two front legs (leaning forward) or on two rear legs (leaning backward). Unlike

Wrong way to sit on a plastic chair

wooden or iron chairs, the legs of plastic chairs are not strong enough to carry the total weight on two legs. So, sitting in this posture on a plastic chair should be avoided. It also carries the risk of falling down, because the plastic legs do not get enough friction from the smooth floor and they slip. Once cracks appear at the junction of the legs and the seat, it quickly spreads and leads to breakage. As there is little scope of repair of plastic things, they should be carefully handled. The other weak point of a plastic chair is the lack of friction between the bottoms of the legs with the surface of the floor. If the surface is too slippery, the legs are likely to get spread away from each other. This weakens the junction. So, plastic chairs are good if they are put on a relatively rough surface like a carpeted surface.

- The weak point of plastic tap is its top part that is rotated to open or close the tap. While using the tap if we solely apply force on the arms, the arms will break quickly. But if we rotate the tap by holding the arms with its axis it will last longer.

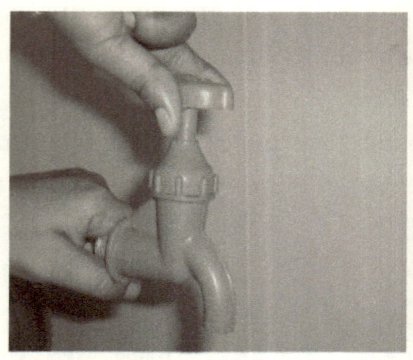 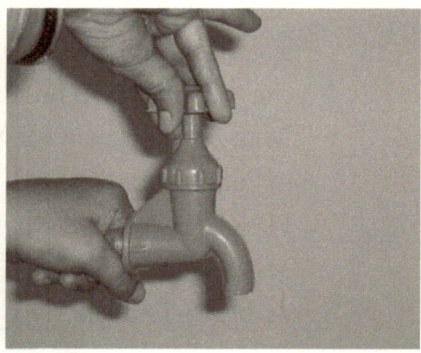

Wrong way to rotate a plastic tap   Correct way to rotate a plastic tap

6. Plastic things lose their luster very quickly. So, we should not buy plastic things for show purpose. If the luster is to be maintained for a longer time, we should not clean them with rough things; nor should we rub them vigorously. They should be cleaned with wet clothes with mild detergents.

13

TAKING CARE OF MACHINES

In every house there are some machines. It may vary from a small radio to a costly car. All the machines are to be taken care of properly so that they will last long and will give the best possible services. Some of the principles of handling the machines are as follows.

We should-

1. **Read the user's manual:** Every machine is provided with a user's manual. It should be read thoroughly. Not only the owner should read, but also the person who is actually going to handle the machine must read it. If he/she is not able to read, the facts written in the manual must be clearly explained to him/her. For example, if the maid-servant is going to use the grinder/ washing machine, she should be explained in detail how to use them. At times it may be required to remind her/him repeatedly. Similarly, if a driver is going to drive the car, he must be explained the user's manual of the car. Not only it has to be read but also it should be properly preserved, so that it can be referred to later on, particularly for troubleshooting.

2. **Use as much as possible:** Machines work well when they are used frequently. If left idle, different parts do not function properly. After some time, these need unnecessary repair and give trouble at the time of need. The machine should be used maximum during the guarantee period, because any defect detected during this period can be taken care of by the manufacturer.

3. **Checkup periodically:** Machines should be periodically checked up by efficient and reliable mechanic. If any part has already started functioning abnormally, it should be immediately repaired or replaced. By that we can prevent a major damage or a major accident/ trouble while being used. By doing so, we can get the uninterrupted service of the machine. The mechanic should be a reliable and efficient one. If one stays at one place for several years, it will not be difficult to find a reliable mechanic. If someone is new to a place, he should ask several persons in the locality about an efficient mechanic. A suitable lubricant is to be put on most of the moving parts of a machine. So, we should apply lubricant as and when recommended, let it is a table fan or a car.

4. **Avoid over use:** Usually it is mentioned in the user's manual how long the machine can run continuously. Continuous running beyond this time may be harmful for the machine. So, such machines should be put to rest after the recommended time. Often continuous running heats the machine and it is the heat that damages the machine. So, enough time should be given to cool down.

5. **Proper installation:** Certain fixed machines need special installation. This is also mentioned in the manual. We should follow the exact method. Enough cooling space, proper grounding of electrical and electronic appliances and a level surface are some of the requirements for installation.

6. **Minor maintenance:** Everybody should know certain minor maintenance tips. Like putting oil into a table fan, putting distilled water into the battery, timely defrosting of the freeze, cleaning the head of a tape-recorder and so on.

14

PREVENTING DAMAGE TO THINGS

Many things are prematurely damaged due to various factors for which we have to buy the same thing again and again. These are some of the guidelines to prevent damage to our belongings.

(i) Preventing damage by insects-

Insects can damage many household things. To avoid damage by insects, proper care of such things should be taken.

- Things made of wood can be prevented from insects like white-ants by time-to-time checkup and regular use. Keeping them dry will also be helpful.
- Damage of woolen clothes can be prevented if these are kept with mothballs.
- Food items to be preserved for a long time should be properly dried before storing. Presence of moisture leads to damage by insects/fungus.
- We should store things in good quality containers so that insects cannot cut it open and attack. The container should be waterproof. Seepage of water into the container can damage

the things (food or other items). Glass containers are good for many things, but it will be difficult to get big size containers if needed. So, metal containers can be used. It should be remembered that acidic substances should not be preserved in metallic containers as they cause corrosion.

- All things that are kept for a long time should be checked periodically and take necessary measures in right time.
- Prepared food should not be kept open; either they should be kept covered or be kept in the freeze.

(ii) Preventing damage while being transported

Every now and then we take things from one place to another. It may be carrying things from or to the market, carrying things to other's house or for traveling to a new place. Things can get damaged while doing so. So, enough care should be taken while transporting things.

The following aspects should be taken care of while transporting things.

1. The container

We should be sure that we are using a good quality container. It may be a box, suitcase, bag or others. It should be strong enough to hold the things. If it breaks on the way it will cause damage to the things inside it. This not only causes damage to the things, but also puts us in an embarrassing and inconvenient situation. Things will move between themselves if the container is under filled. This may cause damage to the things in it. If we fill too tightly, it may cause damage to the container as well as the contents. Let us see a few examples-

➢ If we fill 5kg sugar in a thin plastic bag it may rupture on the way and the sugar may fall out.

> If we fill fifty kg rice into an old bag, it may hold it, but it may get torn on the way.
> Whenever possible we should use the specified container to transport specified things. For example- specified egg container should be used to transfer/carry eggs.

2. Packing and sealing

Things should be properly sealed or packed before transport. There are several things to be looked after while packing. These are-

> The mouth of a bag should be stitched in such a way that the thread will not break, nor it will get automatically opened. The thread is likely to give way if the bag is packed too tightly.
> Glass goods and other breakable things should be properly packed. The best way to do is to pack them in the original packing material with which it was bought. So, it is advised not to throw away the packing materials, particularly if we are in a transferable job where things are to be transported repeatedly. While unpacking such things, we should see carefully the way it has been packed, so that we can adopt the same method to pack ourselves whenever needed.
> There are some bags, which are fitted with zips. Improper use of the zip can damage it. Often this happens if the bag is tightly full or if the zip is pulled without proper alignment or some loose things (like threads) being trapped in it. If so, we should cut all the loose threads near the zip.
> There are bags fitted with locks. Improper handling of these locks can damage them.
> The bags that are to be carried on the shoulder are often provided with straps. If these straps are not strong enough, it may get torn on the way and the bag may fall on to the ground and the contents may get damaged.

➤ If things are to be transferred in rainy season, extra care has to be taken to prevent things from getting wet.

➤ More importance should be given to costly things while packing and transporting, because damage to one costly thing may cause greater loss than breakage of several cheap things.

3. Loading and unloading

Things can get damaged while loading and unloading. People who do not know our things often do these works. They might be expert in loading some other things, but they might be new to our things. So, we should supervise their work and guide them how to handle each item explaining them what is the content of the pack. Proper packaging prevents damage to things to some extent; still then loading and unloading have to be supervised. Dragging of heavy things on the floor should not be allowed. It can cause damage to the floor as well as to the goods. These should be lifted and transferred from one place to another. In order to avoid this problem, we should see that each pack does not become too heavy. Breakable things should be transported with full concentration. Little lack of care can lead to damage of such things. Transport of such things should be finished in one attempt- from the point of lifting till the point of new placement.

(iii) Preventing damage to hanging things

There are many household things that need to be hung either from a nail or from a hook fixed on the wall or on other things. Some principles are to be followed in this regard.

• Before putting a nail in the wall, we should think whether it is really needed or not. Unless needed we should avoid putting nails on the wall as nails can damage the wall, plastering or the painting.

- If decided to put one, then we should think the type of nail or hook to be used. This depends on the purpose of it. If a heavy thing is to be hung, the nail must be sufficiently strong and must have gone sufficiently deep into the wall. Otherwise, it cannot bear the weight of the hanging thing and the hanging thing may fall on to the ground and get damaged/ broken. A small hook may be enough for hanging light objects like a poster or a calendar.
- Now-a-days plastic hooks are available which can be glued to different surfaces and can serve the purpose of a nail. It is not required to hammer into the wall. So, the walls are not damaged. But these hooks may not hold firmly to the surface, particularly if the wall is lime plastered. Once it comes out it disfigures the wall and the same hook may not stick to any other surface easily. However, they can be reutilized by fixing them with stronger adhesives.
- Sometimes we hang bags containing several things. Before doing this, we should check the strength of the bag also; whether it can bear the weight of the content or not.

15

PREVENTING LOSS OF THINGS

Often, we lose things due to lack of proper attention or due to carelessness. So, we have to buy those things again. Hence, we should always try to prevent loss of our belongings. The man who gets the lost things may not gain. Because, he might not be knowing what it is and what is its use? Loss for any reason leads us to buy the thing again which puts pressure on natural resources. Hence, we should prevent loss. These are some of the guidelines to prevent loss.

Let us discuss a few general points before going to a few individual things and how to prevent their loss.

(A) Causes of losing things and methods to prevent-

1. **Forgetting where kept (Misplacement):** We have many things in our house or in our office. But often we forget where we kept it, so that it is not found at the time of need and we have to buy it again. Not only we have to buy it again, but also, we waste time in searching for it. Sometimes this might happen in an odd hour so that it may not be possible to buy it immediately, thereby the work is to be kept pending

till the next day. At times the same thing may not be available at all. In summary loss of things leads to more expenditure and more troubles. The basic cause is misplacement. So, one should keep things in specified sites. Where to keep what, depends on how often we use it and it also needs some scientific knowledge. Let us see some examples.

- Seasonal things are used only in a particular season. For example, the winter dresses, gloves, mufflers etc. are needed in the winter season only. So, they all should be kept in one place. Because these are to be brought out only once in a year, they can be kept in a box. The box need not be kept in an accessible location. Keeping here and there not only can cause loss but also can lead to damage by rodents/insects.

- Writing materials and other stationeries are used almost daily. So, they should be kept in an easily reachable place.

- Things that are required in emergency situations (torch, a stick etc.) must be kept in such a place that it can be obtained easily, even in darkness.

- The books, which we need every now and then, can be kept on our table or on an easily accessible rack. The less used books can be kept inside a box or on a less easily accessible rack.

- A walking stick should be within the reach of the person who uses it. Misplacement may cause a fall of the user and injury.

While keeping things we should carefully choose which place will be ideal for which thing. Whatever may be the thing or wherever we may keep it, we should always use the same place for the same object, so that it becomes a habit. By that we will not forget easily. It becomes easy to get it by all the family members or all the office staffs (in case of office).

2. **Leaving things in the work place:** We take different things out of our house for its use and often forget to bring it back. Often, we leave the thing at the workplace after the work is over. For example, we take the knife to cut some unwanted plants in the garden and often we forget to bring the knife back. On subsequent occasions when we will need it, we will not be able to find it. Even it may not be possible to recollect where we have kept it. To prevent such loss, we should check the work place after the work is over.

3. **Right thing in right place:** Certain things are to be kept in its proper place so that the chances of losing it can be minimized. For example, the spectacles should be over the eyes; the pen should be in the pocket, money in the money purse, stethoscope (for a doctor) over the shoulder. If we habitually keep our purse or keys in a particular pocket, we will be able to detect its loss (if at all) at the earliest.

4. **Try not to get diverted:** Often people try to keep us engaged or try to divert our attention from our belongings in different ways and rob of our things. This particularly happens in public places. So, always we should keep our attention on our belongings, particularly if we are carrying valuable things. In these places we should avoid other's suggestion/advice. Often unsocial people try to help us in different ways to become friendly to us with the intention to rob us at the earliest possible occasion. We should not seek their help. In fact, we should not rely too much on these temporary friends.

5. **Losing things in the train:** Often we lose things in the train. This may be due to carelessness or may be due to theft. That we have to take care of our own belongings while on journey, need not be overemphasized. Some of the guidelines are given here to prevent such occurrences. We should-

- o Try to minimize luggage (travel light). Fewer luggage will get better attention.
- o Try to make one/few big luggage rather than having many small luggage. It is easier for others to pick up a small luggage than a big one.
- o Not open the bags repeatedly. Something may drop out and get lost. To avoid that, things that we need during the journey should be packed separately.
- o Put our own lock to fasten the luggage.
- o If we have hired a porter, we should be always with him. We should not allow him to move too far away from us.
- o Not eat anything from our co-passengers, particularly if they are new to us or freshly known to us. We should never get carried away by their sweet words, whatever faithful words or whatever words of friendship they might tell.
- o Not take outside food. It may not be hygienic also. If at all we need, we should get them from the official vendors.
- o Keep our shoes well deep under the seat when not in use, otherwise we should wear them. If at all we put off, it is better to keep them near the wall, not near the passage.
- o Count our luggage before leaving the train or the platform.
- o While using toilet inside the train often people take out their wallet, watch or mobile phone and keep them on the provided space. While returning from the toilet, we should see that we have not left anything. If our destination has come nearer, we should try to avoid using toilet, because in a hurry we may forget to check our things.

6. **Avoid break journey:** If we are journeying with valuables, we should try to avoid break journey. More frequently we break our journey more likely we would lose things. It is ideal to move from point to point. For example, if we withdraw money

from the bank, you should straight go to our house. Similarly, if we are carrying money to deposit in the bank, we should directly go to the bank without stopping at any other place.

7. **Be careful about giving things to others:** Often many people ask things from us, but quite often they forget to return it. It may be a small thing like a needle or a costly thing like some of our valuable documents. If long time passes away, we might forget to whom we had given it. This amounts to loss of the thing. Some of the steps to prevent such occurrence are-

- We can deny to give from the beginning if we know that the man is not reliable.

- If somebody asks for some important document, we should never give the original. We should ask him to get a Xerox copy done immediately and return the original to us. It will be still better if we ourselves get a Xerox copy done and give it to him.

- If we give something to somebody, we should keep it noted in our notebook and remind him repeatedly.If he does not respond to your reminder, we can go to his residence to get it back. If he returns it is all right, if he cannot return, he will feel offended and will never dare to ask something from us again. If he wants to replace the lost thing, we may or may not accept depending on our personality, cost of the thing, and the overall relationship with him.

(B) Preventing loss of some specific things-

a. **Key:** It appears to be a small thing, but its loss must be dealt with seriously and quickly. If the key is lost and the person who gets the key and if he knows it is ours, he can use it to take away our object; maybe it is our box, motor cycle or others. If it happens to be the key of our house, the man now has total access to our house. So, we must change the lock immediately. Depending on the situation we may inform the police also. Even if we have got the duplicate key, it is not advisable to use the same lock. However, the duplicate key is very useful on other occasions. These days thieves are able to open the key of the two wheelers and take away the bike. To prevent such theft, one should put extra lock. Ideally all keys should be kept at one place. By that we will not forget where we have kept the keys. It will be easy to get the key at the time of need. Similarly, while we are on outside tour, we should keep the keys at one particular place (bag/pocket). If we are keeping in a bag, it should be kept with us all the time. The duplicate keys should be kept away from the originals.

b. **Purse (wallet):** Often people lose their wallet. The wallet usually contains money, credit cards/ debit cards and a few papers. Often the pickpockets steal them. People have a tendency to keep the wallet in their back pocket. It is easier to take away the wallet from the back pocket than from the side pocket. This is particularly so in crowded places. At times purses fall out of the pocket, whether kept in the back pocket or in the side pocket. If we are sitting on a moving vehicle for a long time, the wallet may become loose due to vibration, comes to the mouth of the pocket and finally falls out. So, time to time we should check whether the wallet is there safely or not. This is not a problem if we are standing or walking.

c. **Shoes:** Shoes are often lost in places where several people meet and we have to put off our shoes. Such places are at the entrance of a temple or in some one's house where so many people have gathered. In such places there could be exchange of shoes or somebody might steal it away. So, if we feel that shoes have to be taken out, we should not go with new shoes.

It is better to go with an old and poor-quality shoe. If at all we go, we should keep them in the shoe-stand (if it is there). If a suitable shoe-stand is not there, we should keep our left and right shoe at different places; preferably the left one in the right side and the right one in the left side. It will be difficult for someone to exchange/ steal, but it will not be difficult for us to find them out as we ourselves have kept them. How to keep shoes in a train has already been described.

d. **Pens:** Often people take our pen to do some minor writings, but often they forget to return it and we often forget to collect it from them. In these situations, it would be bad to deny giving the pen to others. So, the best way to do both things (helping others to use our pen and not losing the pen) is- we should give the pen but keeping its cap with us. After use the other person will be forced to return our pen, as he cannot keep the open pen in his pocket.

e. **Loose things in shirt pocket:** Often we keep loose things in front shirt pocket like mobile phone or specs. If the pocket is open these things are likely to fall out and are lost or damaged; particularly when we bend down. So, we should try to avoid putting such things in the front pockets.

f. **Cheque books and cards:** If we lose cheque books or cards, we should inform the bank immediately. We can also inform the police.

g. **Cards and codes:** These-days people are using different types of debit and credit cards. We should not keep the card and code together. We should try to avoid the code number, which others can guess easily. Frequently the code should be changed.

h. **Things inside the car:** We should not keep valuable things inside the car. It is not impossible to open the doors of a locked car. People can break open the car window if they are able to know that valuable things are there inside the car.

SECTION-D

DISPOSAL

16

REPAIR

Due to several reasons our acquired things will get damaged one day or the other. Before throwing them out, we should see if these things can be repaired. But often we try to manage with the damaged thing and delay repair. This is either due to negligence or due to over-confidence. However, mechanical things should be repaired as early as possible. Because continued use of the damaged article may lead to further damage. A minor defect may lead to a major defect. It may require more money to repair. At times it may not be possible to repair at all. The proverb "Stitch in time saves nine" is very much applicable in such situations. It may so happen that the machine stops functioning totally when we needed it most (say in an emergency situation). Not only we face difficulty, but also pay more for repair. So, all things that are not working well should be repaired at the earliest. If the article cannot be repaired at all or it will be too costly to repair; a new one may be bought. Let us discuss a few examples.

- A vehicle shows some starting problems. If we do not repair immediately, it may completely stop on the way and may not restart at all. If we are going for some urgent work, we cannot go and our important work cannot be done. Missing such a work may cost us much more than the cost of repair of the vehicle. If we would have repaired it earlier, it would have cost us less and we would not have faced the problem.

- Suppose there is a breach in the fence in the corn-field of a farmer. If the farmer does not repair it quickly, stray animals can get in and can cause a lot of damage to his crops.

- Suppose we had an umbrella. It was not functioning properly, but we delayed in repairing it, may be that the rainy season was over. But if an untimely shower of rain comes, it would not be possible to use the umbrella. If we would have repaired soon after it was damaged, this situation could have been averted.

- Let us think that we had a coat. One of its buttons was lost in an earlier occasion. But we did not put a new one immediately. If for some reason we wanted to put on this coat, it would not be possible. The cost of a button is nothing in comparison to the service we are deprived of. At times we may have to face embarrassing situation for such minor problems in our dress.

- Suppose there is a small tear in our cloth. If we quickly stitch it up, we may be able to use it for several months. But if we leave it like that and continue to use it, the tear may enlarge and it may not be possible to stitch it. If at all done, it may not be usable. Obviously, it would not look nice.

- Leakage of water from any source must be sealed immediately. If not done, with the progress of time the leak will increase and it can cause damage to several things, like the wall, the wooden goods and the metal goods.

- Electrical goods if not repaired immediately may be responsible for a disaster. It may cause life threatening situations including fire.

In conclusion it can be told that **having a non-functioning thing or a malfunctioning thing is equivalent to or worse than not having**

the thing at all. So, if we have a thing, we should see that it is in a functioning state.

While repairing we should get it done by efficient hands. However, we can repair certain things ourselves. It may not be possible to repair the thing completely, but its further damage can be delayed or prevented. Let us see some examples.

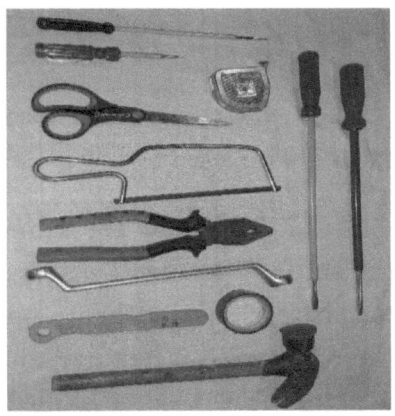

A set of house-hold tools

Self-repair- A set of instruments are required for this purpose. Some of the instruments required are- Screw- drivers of different sizes, wrenches of different sizes, Taster, Pliers, Hammers, drill machine etc. We should know how to use these instruments. Initially we should take enough precaution, so that we do not get hurt. After a few attempts we can use them fairly well. If we closely observe while our things are being repaired by a mechanic, we can learn some basic principle of repairing. We can use this knowledge on subsequent occasions.

Managing with repaired article means we avoided purchasing new things; thereby we decreased load on raw materials. This helps in conserving the environment.

17

REUSE

Before throwing away any thing we should think how the same thing in total or in parts can be reutilized. It is possible on many occasions. This will reduce demand on new things and hence on natural resources. It will be better if we ourselves can reutilize the used things. At times we have to take the help of some skilled persons. If the material cannot be used at all, we should give them to others (vendors) for recycling. Let us discuss a few examples.

(a) Screws, nuts, nails

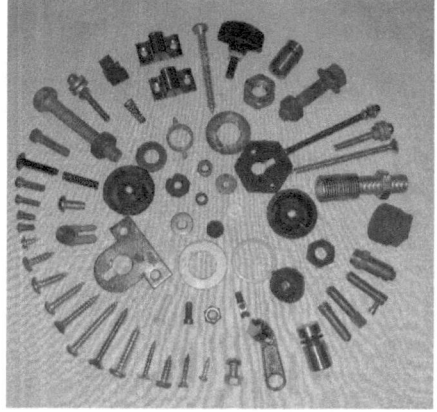

Small but useful things preserved properly

Many domestic things are made up of these types of things. When a machine/article breaks these things are obtained as loose parts. Instead of throwing them out as a whole, we should take out the loose parts and preserve them in a container. These can be utilized at other times. Just to replace a screw or a nut we need not have to go to a mechanic. If we have all these things, we can try ourselves before taking the help of a mechanic. At times by assembling several loose parts we can make a completely new useful item. To use them properly we should have some equipment with us as described earlier.

(b) Ropes and threads

Like the nuts and screws, ropes and threads are required in every household. One can buy new ropes or threads from the market, but often we get them while buying other things used to pack them. We can carefully open them and preserve, so that these can be utilized while packing other things. But while preserving them we should be sure that they do not get matted. To prevent matting, they can be preserved carefully.

Loose threads preserved properly

(c) Clothes

We should not throw away the torn cloths. They can also be sold. Torn cloths can be reused for different purposes. Mattresses can be built from them by stitching several layers of cloths. The mattresses so prepared are truly better than the readymade mattresses available in the market. These are comfortable to sleep; as well as these are good for our health. They prevent backache. Poor people use them as quilt in winter season too.

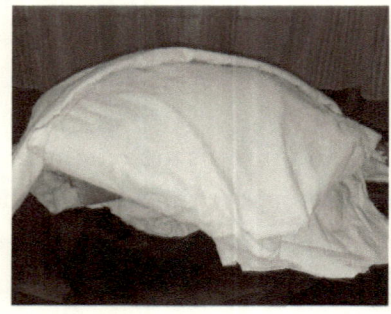
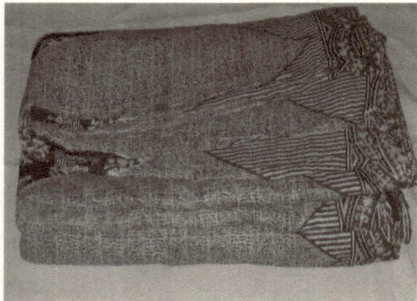

Torn clothes   Torn clothes stitched into a mattress

(d) Kitchen wastes

Kitchen wastes are organic wastes. If these are thrown out here and there, they will putrefy and can cause health hazards. So, instead of throwing out we should bury them in a pit in our backyard. On putrefaction they would produce very good manure, which can be utilized in the kitchen garden. At least some plants can be planted in these pits also. Some of the kitchen wastes are used as food of some animals. If we have one, we can use for their feeding. If we do not have, we can give it to others who have them.

(e) Papers:

We get papers either in the form of newspapers or in the form of school/college copies and old books of school/college going children. Newspapers can be utilized for making covers of the books and copies. Thousands of children in the villages use them for this purpose. Except few interesting articles in the newspaper, other parts can be disposed of by selling to the vendors. In the used copies of children there might some unused pages. The used pages can be sold and the unused pages can be assembled (stitched or pasted) together to make a new copy, which can be used again, at least for rough work.

Loose papers   Loose papers bound
                                to prepare copies

(f) **Wooden products-** Parts of a damaged wooden article can be taken out to be used in smaller wooden article provided the condition of the wood is good. Though there is nothing to worry about small or damaged wooden goods as nature has got its method of recycling (these are biodegradable). However, throwing away useful wooden article will increase demand on woods and will finally lead to cutting of the trees.

18

RECYCLE

Introduction:

Under what circumstances the earth developed has been a matter of speculation to many. Possibly it started from the Sun. The Sun is made up of two main elements hydrogen and Helium. Hydrogen has one proton and one electron. Helium has two protons and two electrons. Hence, to start with the earth also must have only these two elements. But with changing situation, particularly with change of temperature, these electrons and protons joined together to produce the 120 elements now available on earth. Later on, different elements combined with each other to produce different compounds with so many complexities. This is how the nonliving things evolved on earth surface. Every element has its own property though all are made up of the same fundamental particles; electron, proton and neutron. Similarly, all the compounds have their own properties. Under no circumstance they change their property. For example, hydrogen behaves as hydrogen, not like any other element. Oxygen behaves as oxygen, not like any other element. When they combine to form water (a compound), both of them lose their properties. Water gains its new properties, which are completely different from its constituent atoms; hydrogen and oxygen.

The situation under which life appeared on earth is also a mystery. The simplest form of life is a cell. In a cell there are so many molecules arranged in a specified manner to do specified functions. For proper functioning all the bio-molecules should be present in right place. Molecules not properly located cannot do its function. For example, a molecule that is present in the mitochondria, if present in the cytoplasm will not do its function. Hence, in all life forms arrangement of different molecules (anatomy) is very much essential for their proper functioning. Once life entered into a set of compounds a living being was produced. The set of compounds, their amount and their location in an organism are decided by its genetic makeup. With a fixed genetic makeup, a fixed set of compounds will be produced and they will be distributed in a fixed pattern. When all the arrangements are proper a particular life form appears. Every life-form (a conglomeration of molecules) had fixed properties. These properties are nothing but its behavior. The miracle of living forms is that they exist only for a limited period, the life span. Then they die. Once the life force goes out of the body, all materials in it are converted again into simpler compounds or elements by the natural forces and processes. These elements are reutilized to produce new life forms. Some are left as such in nature as elements/ compounds for an indefinite period. Once they are converted to elements or simpler compounds it will not be possible to trace the original source, plant/ insect/ reptile/mammal or others.

Non-living things get changed to newer things by chemical reactions. The chemical reaction takes place under a particular temperature, pressure, presence/ absence of other substances; particularly air and water. A matter with large mass is converted into smaller pieces and particles by natural forces. These natural forces are rain, sun ray and wind. This process is called weathering. It is this weathering that led to the development of soil. Several types of elements and compounds are held together in the soil. Co-existence of several elements and compounds together helped in the development of life forms; particularly the plants to start with. The whole animal kingdom is dependent on plants for food and oxygen. Thus, soil is essential for sustenance of life. No soil- no plants; no plants- no animals. After death all the constituents of the living beings will be converted in to simpler compounds or elements. This means one day all living beings will be converted into non-living things; elements or compounds. These simpler compounds and elements are reutilized for production of newer compounds which are incorporated in to new life forms. The most important component of living organism is carbon, an element with atomic number 6 (6 electrons and 6 protons). The carbon which belongs to grass today will become a part of a cow tomorrow and yet after some days it will become a part of a man or a dog. The vice versa is also true. During life also, certain materials within the living body are also recycled. For example- the life span of RBC (red blood cells) is 120days. After this period, the RBC dies. The compounds like proteins or elements like iron that are released after death of the RBC are transferred to bone marrow where they are reutilized to produce new RBCs. Sometimes the broken-down materials during life are utilized to produce new things; not necessarily the same thing from which it is derived. For example, in an unfed state (when the body is deprived of calories for a long time) the muscle proteins which are basically produced from amino acids are broken down to organic acids (new substance) which can be used to produce energy. Even reutilization takes place within a single cell also. The damaged intra-cellular materials are broken down into simpler substances by lysosome, a cell organelle. These simplified materials are reutilized to produce new organelles.

Studying these natural processes, we can conclude that recycling is the law of nature. The amount of matter on earth has remained constant for millions of years. Utilizing all these matters the nature has nurtured so many living beings including human beings over all these years. New species might have come up but the materials in them are same. Nature has reutilized all the matters. There are many natural cycles like nitrogen cycle, carbon cycle, water cycle, recycling of energy and so on. In other words, nature has not wasted anything on the earth surface. By law of nature there should not be shortage of things if we take the exact amount for our requirement (need) from her. Deficiency occurs only when we want to get more than our requirement (greed). Recycling things will prevent shortage of natural resources. Hence, we all should try to recycle things as much as possible. The recycling method we will use may not be as efficient as the nature does. In fact, the shortage of several things now we face is mainly because we are not able to recycle them properly. As discussed in the beginning of this book if we can limit our need, obviously there will be excess of things in the nature. Limiting one's requirement is as per the law of nature, demanding more is against the law of nature. In addition to limiting our requirement if we can recycle things, we can reduce demand on the natural resources and by that we can save the environment. Saving the environment will save the earth.

I have already mentioned that nature never wastes anything. It recycles all things to keep the creation moving. For nature the concept of disposability does not exist. However, to be available for recycling the element/compound must be present in proper place; must be exposed to natural forces. As a part of the living system the man is supposed to help the nature in the recycling process. Man must be the part because only man is responsible for altering the environment; no other animals have caused the deterioration of the environment. Some products produced by man have been considered as non-recyclable like plastics and glass. But there must be a natural process for their destruction and recycling. It may be physical process or chemical process. The chemical process might be mediated by some microbes. When nature will require the elements from these so called non-biodegradable articles, it will produce a method to convert them to simpler things or elements. Let us take the example of plastics- plastics are basically carbon compounds. Carbon is an essential element for all living organisms. If a huge amount of carbon is trapped in plastics (not recyclable), there will be deficit of carbon for living organisms. If nature wants to keep all the living beings intact, it has to find out a method to extract carbon from plastic. If it cannot, some life forms are bound to suffer and, in the process, they may become extinct. Similarly, if we want to help the nature to keep the life forms intact, we must know how to recycle things. Once some species are extinct it will be difficult to predict what net impact will be in the nature. Because, different life forms are inter-dependent. Some elements may not be required for certain life forms. But they form a part of the environment. A suitable environment is also required for the living beings to survive. Once the environment changes it may not be possible for living beings to thrive in the changed environment. Hence, to maintain the environment in a suitable state for living, we must also handle the non-essential elements with care (to help other creatures).

Let us discuss a few recycling processes taking place in nature.

(a) **Carbon cycle**- Carbon is the most abundant element in living beings; plants or animals. About 47% of the dry weight of living organism is carbon. The most abundant site of carbon is ocean. Mostly it is carbon dioxide in a dissolved state. Then it enters into the sea plants. From sea plants it moves into small fishes; from them to big sea fishes and from big sea fishes to other sea creatures. After death of these animals, carbon in the form of carbon dioxide is returned back to atmosphere. From atmosphere it returns back to ocean water. The other path of carbon cycle is burning of fossil fuel or burning of plant or animal products. They release carbon dioxide. Decomposition of plant or animal products also produces CO_2. The other fate of carbon dioxide released into atmosphere is being taken up by plants to produce monosaccharides like glucose or fructose. Plants produce them by the process of photosynthesis. Large scale cutting down of the trees (deforestation) has been a part and partial of civilization. This can lead to inadequate removal of CO_2 from atmosphere. This is the cause global warming. This is harmful for the earth. If we want to save the earth we have to prevent cutting of plants. This will be possible only by reducing demand on plant products (already discussed). The matter of concern is plastic. As plastic goods are not biodegradable (means not being converted to reusable form of carbon), we must reduce the use of plastic (already discussed).

The steps that can be taken to maintain the carbon cycle are-

- We should try to reduce the use of plant products (Reduce).
- Maintain the wooden goods in such a manner that it will give you service for a long time (prolonged use: discussed earlier).
- Not to depend too much on plastic goods. If we have got some plastic goods, we should use them for a long time. Hence it will not be required to throw them out to environment early (discussed earlier).
- Reuse the wood. That means once a wooden thing is broken, we should try to reutilize in making other things instead of subjecting it for burning or decomposition (already discussed).

(b) Nitrogen cycle: Proteins and nucleic acids are essential components of all life forms. Both these molecules contain nitrogen. In nature nitrogen is abundantly present in air. Very small amount is present in the top layers of soil. Nitrogen from air comes to earth during lightening. Nitrogen is converted in to oxides of nitrogen and getting dissolved in rain water it comes to earth. In this form it enters into plants. Burning of fossil fuel, industrial combustion also produces some oxides of nitrogen. These oxides are converted into ammonia or nitrates by specific micro-organisms present in soil. These are nitrogen fixing bacteria. These nitrates are absorbed in to the plant and then moves up in the food chain. After the death of living organisms or burning of dead parts of organism, nitrogen is returned back to atmosphere. Nitrates from soil can be directly converted to nitrogen by denitrifying bacteria.

(c) Water cycle- Life on earth is possible only due to availability of water. Though three fourth of earth surface is covered with water, but only a little is available on land. Water from any source evaporates to atmosphere. From atmosphere it comes down to earth as rain. This rain water flows down through streams to rivers and from rivers it goes back to ocean (the main reservoir of water). Hence rain is the major source of water on land. If we want to utilize more fresh water, we must conserve the rain water. The rain water is required for land plants and all land animals including man. Methods to conserve water at domestic level and community level have already been discussed.

(d) Phosphorus cycle- Phosphorus in the major component of all cell membranes. We know that cell is the unit of life. Hence phosphorus is also an essential component of living beings. The main source of phosphorus in nature is rocks where it is present as phosphates. In the process of weathering, it enters in to the soil. From soil it gets absorbed by plants and then reaches various plant products. From there is moves up in the food chain. With death of the organism, it is retuned back to the nature. Now it is available for reutilization.

Thus, we can conclude from these four examples that in nature there are different cycles by which same element or compound is recycled again and again. For this there is no shortage of them. It is the human activities that have altered the natural cycles resulting in shortage of some substances and excess of some substances. At times certain substances have accumulated too much and they are not available for recycling (like plastic). Shortages or excess leads to altered environmental status which becomes harmful to certain species of organisms. Human being also suffers. If the process continues, the earth may become inhabitable for some life forms. If we follow the laws of nature (recycling) and practice in our daily life, we can keep the earth habitable for a long period of time.

Recycling can be classified in to the following categories.
  (i) Recycling in total
  (ii) Macro recycling
  (iii) Micro recycling

(I) Recycling in total

> If certain thing has gone beyond repair it is to be disposed of. Every country should have its own guidelines for disposal or recycling things. Whatever may be the country-wise rule, some basic rules must be adopted by every country. We know that to construct an article several things are required. All these things are obtained from different sources and then assembled

together to get the article. Hence the manufacturer of the object knows what are the materials required and from which sources they were obtained. If a damaged article is returned back to the manufacturer, he can better help in sending each of these items to its corresponding producer. Now the primary producer of that thing can decide how to reuse the same thing or it has to be sent to the raw material processing unit to repeat the whole process. If we adopt this method, very few things will be wasted and majority of the things will be reused.

Let us discuss about a car. A car is primarily made up of steel which comes from steel industry. There are rubber goods (gaskets, tires and mats) which come from rubber industry. There are electric wires which are made of plastic insulation with copper or aluminum wires. There are glass goods like bulbs, windscreen and windows panes which come from glass industry. There are also many plastic materials obtained from plastic industries. The car industry can be considered as secondary industry. The other industries that provided these materials for making the car can be considered as primary industries. The primary industries get raw materials from plants, animals or minerals. If a car goes beyond repair it should be recycled as a whole. Ideally it should be sent back to the car industry. There its various parts can be dismantled and different parts should be sent back to those primary industries from where they were obtained at the time of manufacture. Even some parts may be directly utilized by the car industries. By this majority of the parts can be recycled and very little things will be wasted.

Let us discuss it in the form of a diagram.

In this type of recycling the flow is from **raw material→ primary industry→ Secondary Industry→ Show rooms → Customers→Show** room→ **Secondary Industry→ Primary Industry.** It may not be possible for these types of goods to return back to the raw material stage. As it is not possible to return back to the raw material stage naturally or artificially, all such goods must be maximally recycled otherwise a day will come when there will be shortage of raw materials. These are mostly the minerals. Neither naturally nor artificially it will be possible to make minerals. The only exception may be volcanic eruptions which may produce some minerals. Almost all metallic goods must be subjected to recycling. This will reduce burden on mining and hence preserve the natural environment. Whole article recycling like that of car is possible for few more articles like personal computers, laptops, mobile phones, refrigerators, washing machines, printers where different types of materials are used in the same machine.

Things made up of single materials like steel can be recycled in this way also, but it takes a shorter route of recycling. Just sending back to the primary industry will solve the purpose. Plastic goods, iron goods, brass goods can be recycled in this manner.

Normal flow of mineral goods-

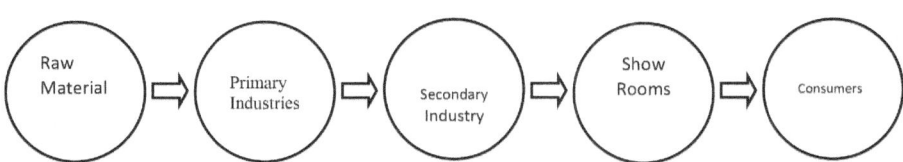

Ideal steps for recycling should end where it started (raw material/ minerals), but it is not possible.

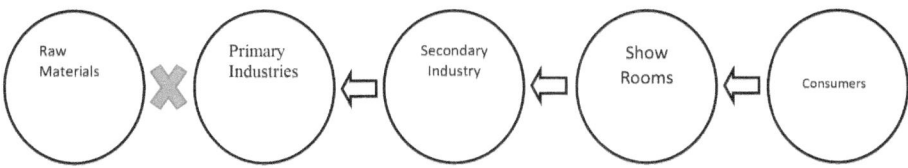

What is possible is-

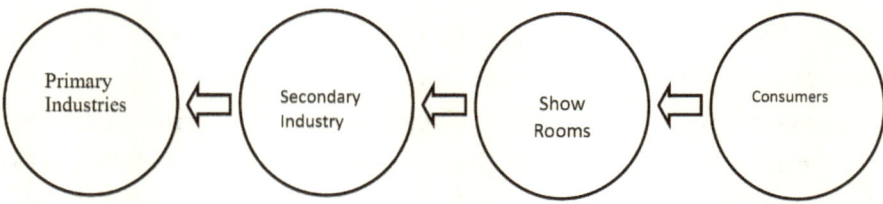

(II) Macro-recycling

Sometimes things are damaged to such an extent that it cannot be recycled in total. Such things should be broken down into parts and each part can be recycled. The customers throw the pieces here and there and the rag pickers gather them and sell to the vendors. Sometimes the customers sell the large parts directly to the vendors. The vendors take the active part in recycling. The smaller pieces are at times so small that even the rag pickers fail to find them. Such pieces are lost forever. This type of recycling is continuing in country like India. This is an unregulated way of recycling. There is no proper channel, there is no proper pricing of the recycled items. As the customers do not get much on majority of the occasions, they do not take much interest in recycling. So, the existing method of recycling must be streamlined. Every Government must regulate and encourage recycling by this method. Then only we can save many metals and a few non-metals also (like rubber). Most of the materials collected in this manner do not reach the secondary level of industries. Mostly such materials reach primary industries where they are treated as raw materials. But they could have been better utilized if they could have reached the secondary level of industries.

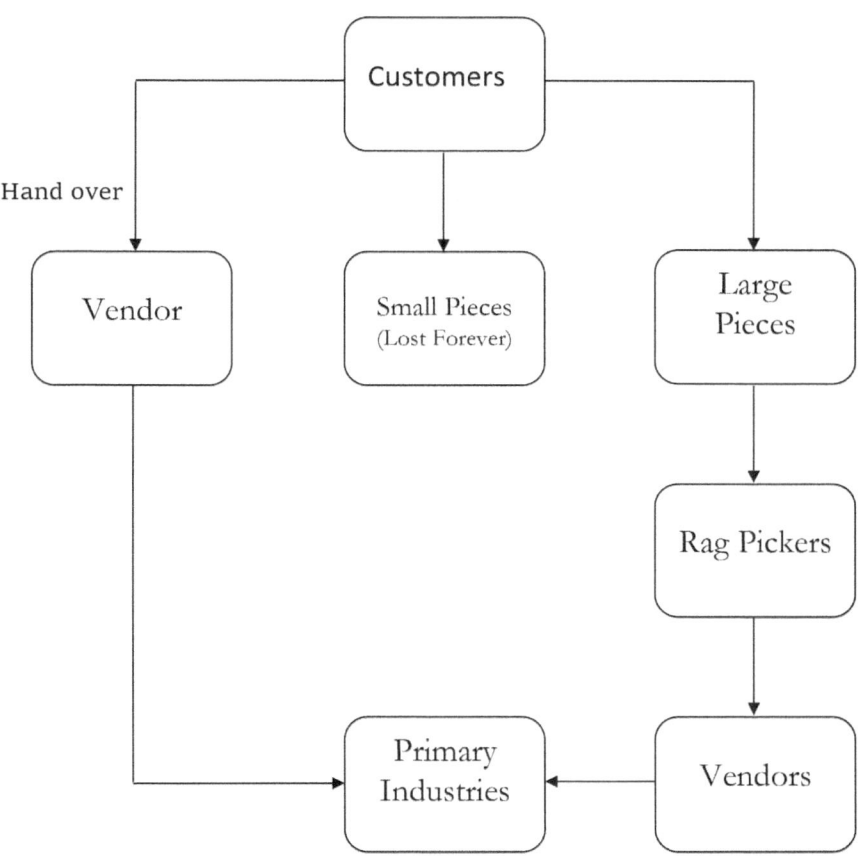

Ideal recycling should be Customers→Show rooms (from where it was bought)→Secondary Industries {may be reused} or → Primary Industries. Recycling in this process will cause little wastage. The responsibility of recycling should be with the producing industries.

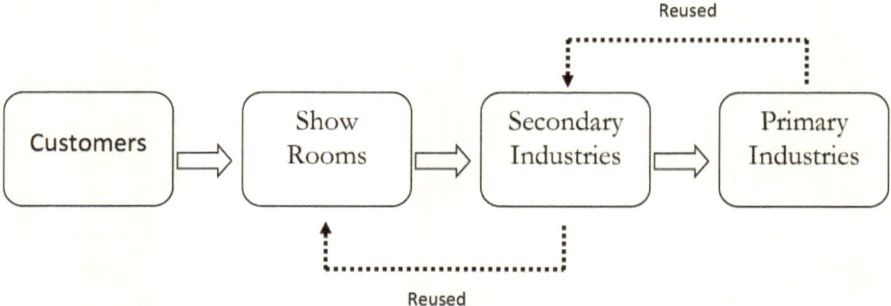

The articles which are recycled in this manner are too heavy or too big. It becomes impossible on the part of the customers to keep them within their premises for a long time. So, they are forced to sell these items to the vendors at a cheap price. Examples of such items are broken gates, broken parts of vehicles, broken utensils and broken parts of other house-hold things or machines.

Let us discuss recycling of a few individual things.

Plastic goods

Plastic goods once broken are difficult to repair. However, under certain situations they can be repaired by using strong adhesive. By that the article will serve the purpose, but it will not look nice. More often these are thrown away. But instead of throwing away we should sell them to proper vendors for recycling. One should not burn the plastic goods as they generate dangerous fumes that can cause cancer. We can keep a sac to store all the small or big plastic goods so that we can sell them once, instead of selling the small ones separately.

Metal goods

Many metal goods are repairable. We should try to repair them by suitable welding. If they cannot be repaired, they can be sold to proper vendors instead of throwing them out. At times we can buy new things in their exchange. The method described above to keep all damaged things in one place can be adopted here also, as it may not be possible to sell small things at a time.

We should be very clear in our mind why we are recycling things. We should not think that it is a source of earning, rather by doing so we are doing good to the whole world; we are helping to preserve the resources on our planet and maintaining a healthy environment.

(III) Micro recycling

Maximum loss of materials occurs at this level. These are small things; some are very small; may be in milligrams. If we sell them, we will not get any price. Even the rag pickers do not collect them. At times they cannot collect them. Once thrown out, such things are lost forever. These things might look too small, but the total amount generated worldwide will be a huge amount. So, attempts should be made to prevent loss of such things and make them available for recycling. Let us discuss a few examples. Small pieces of papers, a piece of electric wire, a broken electrical gadget, few stapler pins, the aluminium covers of medicine stirps, pins, few metallic nails and many others. All these things possess valuable metals like iron, copper or aluminium or some alloy like brass. These things can be and should be recycled. It is possible to recycle these small apparently value less things. Steps to encourage recycling of such things should be taken. The steps are (i) Making common people aware of the value of recycling these things and (ii) Creating centers of micro recycling.

A micro-recycling Unit

The first step can be achieved by advertisement by all the governments in printed and electronic media.

The second requirement is a micro recycling center. A typical recycling center should have the following features.

> Micro recycling centers should be established in different parts of the cities and important parts of rural areas like the village markets.
> These centers will have separate containers to keep separate metal items like iron, brass, tin, zinc, aluminium, lead, copper and so on. One miscellaneous container should be there to keep unknown metal or alloy item.
> The owner should be trained how to identify the metals or alloys. So that he will keep them in the respective container.
> There has to be a physical balance which can weigh very light articles; may be in milligrams.
> People can deposit in these centers whatever small articles they can and as many times as possible.
> There should be registers in the center mentioning the name or identification number of the depositor.

➤ Each time a person deposits a metal, it is weighed and recorded in the register against his name. There should be different columns for different metal/alloy items for each customer.

➤ Payment will be done once his deposit of a particular metal exceeds certain grams depending on the type of metal or alloy. For example, 500gms for iron, 100gm for copper, 250grams for brass and so on.

➤ Once the customer gets the price of his materials his account for that metal is to be closed and the new calculation sheet will start. The customer has to sign the register to avoid future confusions.

➤ Children will be inclined to adopt this type of recycling.

19

NON-RECYCLABLE THINGS

Certain things cannot be recycled at all. Like broken bricks, plastered cements released at construction site, industrial debris, and certain plastic and glass goods. These non-recyclable things should be properly disposed of as recommended in different municipal areas. They should be dumped in such a way that neither they will bring damage to land nor should they obstruct the passage of water flow. The best way to utilize them is to use in filling low-lying lands or in constructing roads. Heavy rollers can crush them and can make them compact.

20

DISPOSABILITY

As we have discussed nature utilizes the same resources again and again. Nothing is disposable for nature. But of late man has developed the concept of disposability. We throw away an article after a single use. This is an absolutely an unnatural concept. Let us discuss a small thing like an injection syringe. We are throwing away the syringes after a single use. What it does- it increases the total cost of treatment and produces a huge amount of hospital waste. Collection and proper disposal have become a cumbersome affair. It involves huge amount of money also. Few years back we were using glass syringes which were being reused after being boiled or autoclaved. This was as per the law of nature. However, some people did not sterilize them properly for which some infections (Hepatitis-B, HIV) spread by such needles or syringes. Here, the fault was not with the principle; rather the fault was with the person and his mentality. For a few persons' mistakes, we should not have changed the principle which was as per the law of nature. By doing so, we are paying the penalty as discussed. The steps being taken to dispose of the used syringes should not have been required. The used syringes should have been taken by the sterilizing system of the hospital or of the community as a whole and after sterilization, they should have been sent for reuse.

It would not have generated the huge amount of waste and would have saved the environment and cost involved.

This method of reuse after proper modification should be applied for many more things. This will be good for nature.

SECTION-E

SAVING ENERGY

21

INTRODUCTION

We discussed how we should use material things so that it will give us service for a long time and help in protecting the earth's environment. The other aspect is the use of energy. We know energy in the universe is constant; it can neither be created nor be destroyed. It can only be transformed. The most important source of energy is the Sun; but the most common form of energy used by us on the earth is the electrical energy. Electrical energy is not produced naturally. Other forms of energy are converted into electrical energy and then it is utilized. It is to be remembered that electrical energy cannot be stored for a long time. Once produced should be used quickly. Production of electrical energy is neither cheap nor convenient. Hence, everybody must know how to use it properly. Wastage somewhere may result in deficiency elsewhere.

Lot of energy is there in the muscles of men and animals. In the earlier days this was the most common form of energy to be used. Muscular energy is a form of chemical energy. With the development of so many machines hardly muscular energy is being used now. The unutilized muscular energy of men has led to development of many life style diseases like obesity, diabetes mellitus, hypertension, heart ailments etc.

22

ELECTRICAL ENERGY

Merits-

- Is easily converted to other forms of energy.
- Can do very large amount of work.
- Can do a lot of work within a short time.

Demerits-

- Its production is costly.
- It cannot be conserved for a long time.
- It can pollute the environment at times (usually at the time of production of thermal power).
- It cannot be easily reproduced. The whole process is to be repeated. For example, electrical energy is utilized to glow bulbs, but we cannot produce electrical energy efficiently from a glowing bulb.
- It makes many people unemployed and lazy. This leads to individual and social problems.

Electricity is produced from different sources. These are hydroelectricity from running water, thermal electricity from burning coal or petroleum products, nuclear energy by nuclear reactions (fusion or fission). Whatever may be the source of generation of electricity, it requires some raw material. Producing electricity from raw materials is a cumbersome process. Transmission of electrical energy is also a costly affair. If we waste electricity we have to produce more. By that we will use more raw materials which is likely to be harmful to the environment. As such it wastes national wealth also. Hence, electricity should be conserved by all by using them properly and rationally. Almost in every house-hold there are some electrically operated machines or equipment. So, proper knowledge of using electricity is to be learnt by all.

Electricity at domestic level is used in the following devices.

Light	Fan
Grinders	Pump sets
Washing machines	TV
Freeze	Coolers
Water heaters	Heaters
Air conditioners	Ovens

Here are some of the ways to conserve electricity.

- We should utilize daylight to the maximum. For that the houses should be so constructed that every room should be properly lighted. We should develop the habit of getting up early and going to sleep early. We should do maximum work in daytime and don't leave much work for night time. Some people have the habit of working late in the night and getting up late in the morning. It is advisable to change their habit and it is possible to change also.
- We should switch off all the lights and fans when they are not in use. The elders must develop this habit, so that they can teach the youngsters. It is often observed that many people

do not follow this principle in their office; thinking that it is the office that is going to pay the bill. But this is only half truth. Often this bad habit is carried forward to their house also. Besides, wherever it may be, it is wastage of national property. Every member in the family should see that this is followed strictly.

- Some of the electrical equipment are to be constantly used like the refrigerator. Ordinarily such things cannot be switched off, but if not in use for several days, it should be switched off. Refrigerators should be timely defrosted to decrease power consumption. People tend to buy big refrigerators, but one should buy that one which is exactly required for his purpose. Big refrigerators have big ice chambers, which are rarely needed.

- We should know to share the fan and light. This means all family members should try to do their work in the same room, so that fans and light in the other rooms can be switched off. This may not be possible always. Whenever possible it should be practiced. For example, if the children are reading in one room, the parents can do their small work like reading or writing in the same room without disturbing the children. The mother can sew small domestic things or the father can do some writing or reading. Here all share the same light and fan and at the same time the children are kept under supervision.

- We should know that tube lights consume less power than bulb lights. So, we should fit more and more tube lights in our house. Tube lights do not raise the room temperature as done by bulb lights. If there is low voltage it is wiser to use voltage stabilizers to use the tube lights. If one does not feel comfortable in reading under tube light, he can use table lamps for the purpose. Fluorescent lights are good enough for general lighting, not for reading. These can be used in the toilets and corridors. All these types of lighting materials have been practically replaced by CFL and LED lights. They are more energy conserving than the earlier forms of lights. Hence, we can change over to these lights.

- We should try to use the regulator of the fan. If no regulator is used, the fan will move at its maximum speed which may not be required always. The regulator can be used to regulate the moving speed of the fan and that can save power. Morning is always cool. Many works can be done during this time without the help of a fan. So, we should try to utilize the morning time properly.

- At times it so happens that at the time we leave the house, there was power cut and some of the electrical points might have remained switched on. If power supply is established after we left, all those electrical equipment will run, thereby consuming electricity unnecessarily. Equipment like heaters/irons may cause fire under such situation. So, we should make it a point to switch off all the electrical points before locking our door, every time.

- Similar situation might happen at night. We go to sleep while there was no power supply. But after we are asleep, the power supply gets established, and the light and fans start working throughout the night. So, before going to bed we should be sure that all the electrical points are switched off, daily. Some light points may be kept switched on, like those in the toilets or staircase. If at all such lights are kept on, it should be of low wattage.

- Electrical goods like air-conditioners, heaters, geysers, electric irons and pump-sets consume a lot of electricity. So, we should be very judicious in using them. For example, if we are heating water in winter season with an immersion heater, we have to heat a minimum amount of water to maintain the minimum water level. But this much of water may not be required for us. So, we should heat to a less temperature and utilize the whole amount of water instead of heating to a high temperature and utilizing only a part of it. If at all we overheat the water, we should try to use the heated water properly. This can be done if several members of the family use this water in quick succession (say bathing) before the heated water cools down. The heated water should be quickly and completely utilized. If it is allowed to cool down it may be required to heat it again. Similarly, if we are using a heater, we should use it exactly for the required time. At times we remain busy otherwise and in the meantime the heating continues for a long-time causing wastage of electricity and at times wasting the materials being heated also.

- We should use the washing machine intelligently. Every washing machine has got a capacity. We should see that in one sitting we should wash the required quantity of cloth. If we wash less cloth than this, not only it will cause wastage of electricity but also it will lead to wastage of detergents.

- Once we start ironing clothes with an electric iron, we should try to iron as many clothes as possible in one sitting. Ironing the required amount of clothes in one sitting consumes less electricity than ironing them in multiple sittings.

- Calculative use of grinders can also conserve electricity. If we are grinding spices, we should grind more in one sitting and preserve the surplus amount in a freeze. We should see that the grinded spices are utilized within a short time. Otherwise, it will be spoiled.

- If we are using an air conditioner, we should try to set the maximum comfortable temperature. There is no meaning in chilling the room and covering ourselves in blankets. If the occupants in the room are few, temperature setting should be at a higher level than if there are more people. We should see that all the doors and windows are closed properly. We should not open the door repeatedly. In daytime, temperature setting should be at a lower level than at night (depends on the ambient temperature). AC can be completely switched off towards late night.

- Almost every house has a television. There are so many channels in the TV that one will get programs throughout the day. But very few programs are worth seeing. We should select the programs we really want to see and switch on at that time. In many houses, TV continues to run for hours even in the absence of any viewer. Such practice should be avoided. Watching TV without planning leads to wastage of time, wastage of electricity and leads to noise pollution.

These are some of the general guidelines to use electricity by which one can limit the use of electricity.

23

CHEMICAL ENERGY

The most commonly used chemical energy is the muscular energy of man and animals. Here either carbohydrate or fatty acids are chemically converted into simpler molecules to release energy. This energy is utilized by almost all living beings to do different activities. The other types of chemical energy are the batteries or dry cells. Here chemical reactions are utilized to generate electrical energy. Burning of fossil fuel in the form of coal and petroleum products also generate energy. It primarily yields heat energy which can be converted in to light energy, kinetic energy or electrical energy. Burning of fossil fuel generates harmful gases and particulate materials which are responsible for air pollution.

(a) **Muscular energy**- We use our muscles for many daily activities. Before the development of electricity most of our activities were done either by our own muscle power or with the help of animal muscle power. Here chemical energy is converted mostly into mechanical or kinetic energy. Certain heavy or very heavy work cannot be done by this form of energy. But the works that can be done by us or by our animals should not be done by electrical energy. Using our own muscle also protects us from different diseases like diabetes mellitus and heart ailments. Some of the examples are carrying our own luggage, walking short distances, doing all household work manually etc. Similarly, animal power can be used to transport things over short distances. Proper utilization of muscular energy keeps many people engaged; which prevents development of unsocial activities in our community. When electrical energy is used in place of muscular energy, many people become unemployed and unsocial activities in the society rises. Muscular energy is easily replaceable. Once we take food, we are loaded with energy again. It does not require any maintenance. Muscular energy does not pollute environment.

Merits-
- It is easily available.
- It is easily replaceable.
- It does not pollute environment.
- It keeps us physically fit/ helps in maintaining social harmony.
- It does not require maintenance.

Demerit-

- Heavy work cannot be done.
- It takes longer time to complete a particular work.

(b) **Cells/ Batteries**- These are the other sources of chemical energy. Their production is costly and they require maintenance also. Such energy can be stored for a limited period only. So, we should use them in such way that these are not wasted. If it is a rechargeable one, we should recharge them in right time. If not recharged in proper time the energy gets wasted. This form of energy does not pollute the environment.

Merits-

- It is convenient at certain places.
- It does not pollute the environment.

Demerits-

- It works for a limited time.
- It requires maintenance.
- It is costly.
- By this only a limited amount of energy can be obtained.

www.ingramcontent.com/pod-product-compliance
Lightning Source LLC
Chambersburg PA
CBHW020542290526
45786CB00002B/993